W9-AZL-352

THE RUNNER-UP PRESIDENCY

The Elections That Defied America's Popular Will
(and How Our Democracy Remains in Danger)

MARK WESTON

Guilford, Connecticut

To my mother, Marybeth Weston,
who lived to see this book completed, but not published,

And to my wife, Linda Richichi,
who has given me so much love.

An imprint of Rowman & Littlefield

Distributed by NATIONAL BOOK NETWORK

Copyright © 2016 Mark Weston

Map of United States of America with States: Outline by FreeVectorMaps.com

British Library Cataloguing in Publication Information Available

Library of Congress Cataloging-in-Publication Data Available
ISBN 978-1-4930-2257-1 (hardcover)
ISBN 978-1-4930-2258-8 (e-book)

∞™ The paper used in this publication meets the minimum requirements of American National Standard for Information Sciences—Permanence of Paper for Printed Library Materials, ANSI/NISO Z39.48-1992.

Contents

Introduction

Electoral Votes: A Risky Game of Dice

WHEN GEORGE W. BUSH WON THE PRESIDENCY IN 2000 WITH NEARLY 544,000 fewer votes than Al Gore, it was not a fluke. Runner-up candidates became president in 1876 and 1888, and the real surprise is that it took 112 years for this to happen again. Another second-place candidate will probably win the presidency soon—and this time, the outrage will be greater because the public will not see the election's outcome as a rare mishap, but as the product of a flawed political system.

In fact, we nearly had a second-place president in 2012. Because of Bush's victory in 2000, most people think that our electoral system is biased toward the Republicans. But if Mitt Romney had won 2% more of the popular vote in every state in 2012, and President Obama had won 2% less, then Obama would have been a runner-up president in his second term, just as President Bush was in his first term. With the extra votes, Romney would have won the nation's popular vote and taken Florida, Virginia, and Ohio, but President Obama would still have won the other northern swing states, and with them, the electoral vote, 272 to 266.

Are conservatives angry now? Imagine their wrath if President Obama had been reelected president with fewer popular votes than Mitt Romney. And think of the fury Democrats will feel if a Republican runner-up is elected again. Most Democrats accepted the result of the 2000 election when the Supreme Court stopped Florida's recount, but many still have bitter feelings about it.

If a Republican with fewer popular votes than his or her opponent is elected again, the anger repressed since 2000 could poison the political climate. Democrats may be far less willing than before to concede the legitimacy of a second Republican runner-up president. If our democracy does not seem to be working, massive demonstrations and even civil disobedience could become common.

Both here and abroad, people would question whether America is truly a democracy or just pretending to be one. Diplomats serving the next second-place president would have a hard time lecturing dictators about human rights if at home the most basic right of being able to choose one's leader were in question.

In 2000, even though a half a million more people voted for Gore than Bush, the public accepted Bush's victory calmly. First, the 9/11 attacks occurred less than eight months after President Bush's inauguration, confirming his authority as Commander in Chief in a way that the election never had. Patriotism set aside the lingering doubt about Bush's legitimacy.

Second, and more important, the public believed that the 2000 election's strange outcome was a once-in-a-century oddity. America had not elected a runner-up president since 1888—when the Republican nominee, Benjamin Harrison, defeated the Democratic incumbent president, Grover Cleveland, with 90,000 fewer votes. Most Americans continue to assume that nothing like this will happen again for another hundred years.

During a *series* of close elections, however, a runner-up president is a probability, not a rarity. After 1876, for example, when the Republican runner-up candidate, Rutherford B. Hayes, defeated the Democratic popular-vote winner, Samuel Tilden, it took *only 12 years* for another second-place candidate, Benjamin Harrison, to be elected president. Two "flukes" in just 12 years.

In our own time, if the next runner-up president is a Democrat (so that Republicans and Democrats will have *both* shared the pain of feeling cheated by the electoral system), the result might be a rush to replace the electoral system with something new and ill-advised, with unintended and unfortunate consequences.

Those who defend America's nearly 230-year-old system of electoral votes, and who want to preserve the state-by-state basis of presidential campaigns, need to realize that the historic arrangement is in danger. Without some modifications, the electoral system may not survive another runner-up presidency.

Skeptics will ask whether another second-place president will really be elected soon. The answer, regrettably, is yes. When the country is about evenly divided between its two main political parties, as it is now, the electoral system resembles a risky game of dice. Of the 10 elections in American history when one presidential candidate has come within 3% of the popular vote of another (and this includes the 2000 and 2004 elections), the second-place candidate has won the most electoral votes—and the presidency—three times. In short, when an election is close, the chance of a runner-up candidate becoming president is approximately 30%.

Assuming that when the parties are equally balanced only half of the presidential elections will be this close, there is still about a 15% (half of 30%) chance during each election that the runner-up candidate will win.

Even when one party has been dominant, as was true during most of the 20th century, one-sixth of the elections were still quite close. So during a period of one-party supremacy, the chance of a runner-up candidate winning the presidency is still about 5% (one-sixth of 30%). If we split the difference between a 15% chance (when the parties are evenly divided) and a 5% chance (when one party is dominant), there is about a 10% chance in each presidential election that a runner-up candidate will win.

Here are the approximate odds of our country electing another runner-up president:

Cumulative Chances of Electing Another Runner-Up President

in 2016	10%
by 2020	19%
by 2024	27%
by 2028	34%
by 2032	41%
by 2036	47%
by 2040	52%
by 2044	57%
by 2048	61%
by 2052	65%

It is more likely than not that we will elect another runner-up president in the next 30 or 40 years. Without an adjustment, America's two-century-old system of electoral votes will threaten both the legitimacy and effectiveness of future presidents.

But the electoral system does not need to be replaced, only repaired—preferably sooner rather than later. Must we really wait until another runner-up candidate moves into the White House, as a majority of Americans watch the news and sigh, "Not again"?

CHAPTER 1

What Were the Founders Thinking?

The Electoral System's Oddities, Origins, and Benefits

THE ELECTORAL COLLEGE HAS BEEN PART OF AMERICAN LIFE FOR MORE than two centuries, but few Americans can tell you exactly what it is or does. When a Philadelphia reporter once asked a man about the institution, he replied, "Everyone should go to college, and if he or she can't afford Harvard or Yale, why, Electoral is just as good, if you work."

WHAT IS AN ELECTORAL VOTE, AND WHO ARE THE ELECTORS?
Every four years, when we think we are voting for president, we're really voting for one of several competing slates of "electors," each one sponsored by a different political party and supporting that party's presidential nominee. The parties choose their electors at state conventions or by a vote of the state party's central committee. The men and women they select are longtime party workers, donors, or local officeholders, and last-minute substitutes are often state government employees quickly chosen by the state party's chairman. So the grandiosely named "Electoral College" is really a rather obscure group of people.

Under the Constitution, the number of electors a state has is equal to the number of representatives the state has in both the US Senate and House of Representatives. If, for example, a state has one member in the House, like Wyoming, and two senators, it has three electoral votes.

Six weeks after the November presidential election, on the Monday closest to the middle of December, the electors who supported the presidential candidate who won the most popular votes in their state meet in their state's capital city, and often in the state's capitol building, to officially cast their state's electoral votes for president and vice president. The electoral "college" therefore has no single campus, but meets instead in 50 different state capitals. In 21 states, electors can vote for whomever they wish, but even in the other 29 states, the pledges that the electors make in advance to their political parties are probably not legally binding. Still, because presidential electors are nearly always reliable party workers, they have voted for their party's candidates more than 99.9% of the time. Of the roughly 21,700 men and women who have cast electoral votes since 1820, only 11 have spurned their party's nominee.

After a state's electors have cast two separate ballots for president and vice president, the state's governor certifies the results and sends them to the president of the US Senate, who is usually the incumbent vice president of the United States who is finishing his or her four-year term.

Some states with outdated laws pay their electors a fee of 10 dollars a day or less. Other states pay about the same expenses per day that they pay their legislators. The state of Washington, for example, pays its electors $88 a day for lodging, $61 a day for meals, and 56.5 cents per mile for driving.

On January 6, two weeks before Inauguration Day, the US House and Senate meet in a joint session to count each state's electoral votes. The vice president presides over this joint session and announces the nation's final total of electoral votes. Ironically, it was Vice President Al Gore who declared that his opponent, George W. Bush, had won the presidency in January 2001, and Vice President Richard Nixon who announced the victory of his rival, John F. Kennedy, in January 1961.

THE ELECTORAL SYSTEM'S TWO QUIRKS

America's electoral system has lasted more than 225 years because its two quirks, one pro-rural and one pro-urban, usually balance each other out. The pro-rural distortion that benefits sparsely populated states and worked in George W. Bush's favor in 2000 comes from the second paragraph of Article II of the Constitution, which says:

Each State shall appoint, in such Manner as the Legislature thereof may direct, a Number of Electors, equal to the whole Number of

Senators and Representatives to which the State may be entitled in the Congress.

In other words, because every state has two senators, it has two more electoral votes than would be justified by its population alone.

California, for example, has 53 House members and two senators, and therefore has 55 electoral votes. Wyoming, however, the least populated state, has just one House member but still has two senators, so it has three electoral votes, *triple* the number of electoral votes that its population alone would warrant. Vermont, Delaware, Alaska, Montana, North Dakota, and South Dakota also each have one representative but three electoral votes, so like Wyoming, each of these states also has three times more electoral votes than is warranted by its population.

In 2000 this worked in George W. Bush's favor when all of the Great Plains and Rocky Mountain states except New Mexico voted for Bush. Together these 12 Republican states had 36 congressmen but *60* electoral votes, 24 more electoral votes than their population warranted, and these extra electoral votes gave Bush his margin of victory.

But electoral votes also have a pro-urban distortion: the "winner-take-all" method of awarding electoral votes. Since the early 19th century, whoever wins the most popular votes in a state also takes *every one* of the state's electoral votes. Think about this. Not only are the votes for a losing candidate in a state ignored, they are treated as if they had been cast for the winning candidate. In 2012, for example, Mitt Romney won 4.8 million votes in California, but Barack Obama (with 7.9 million votes) received all of California's 55 electoral votes. Similarly, Obama received 3.3 million votes in Texas, but Romney (with 4.6 million votes) won every one of Texas's 38 electoral votes.

In 1992 the elder President Bush won all eight of Arizona's electoral votes even though he received only 38.5% of Arizona's popular vote in a three-way race against Bill Clinton and Ross Perot. Indeed, Perot took 19% of the nation's popular vote that year, but failed to win even one electoral vote because he did not finish first in any state.

By contrast, Bill Clinton won only 43% of the popular vote in 1992, but finished first in 32 states and therefore took 370 electoral votes, nearly

70% of the total. An even more striking example of the winner-take-all system's "magnifying effect" took place in 1984, when President Ronald Reagan, running for reelection against Walter Mondale, took 59% of the popular vote, but finished first in 49 states and therefore won 525 electoral votes (out of 538), 98% of the total.

The winner-take-all system also helped John Kennedy win a large electoral-vote majority over Richard Nixon (303 to 219) in 1960, even though he won the popular vote by just ⅙ of 1%.*

In 1888 the winner-take-all system's distortions allowed the Republican candidate, Benjamin Harrison, to win the presidency with nearly 91,000 fewer votes than his Democratic opponent, President Grover Cleveland, who led with 48.6% of the popular vote that year. Harrison took only 47.8% but won the electoral vote decisively, 233 to 168; though he took four of the most populous states—New York, Ohio, Indiana, and Illinois—by narrow margins, he won *all 96* of their electoral votes.

Could this happen again? Definitely. If the 2016 election is close, and let's say, Hillary Clinton were to win Pennsylvania, Colorado, and Wisconsin by narrow margins, she could easily win the election with fewer popular votes than her Republican opponent.

Under the winner-take-all system, the difference between winning a big state and losing a big state by 1% or 2% of the popular vote is the difference between a president and an also-ran. In 2004, for example, John Kerry won nearly 49% of the vote in Ohio but lost the state to George W. Bush and therefore did not take any of its 20 electoral votes, and the loss of Ohio cost Kerry the presidency. Similarly, in 1976 Gerald Ford won 48% of the vote in New York but lost the state to Jimmy Carter, and the loss of New York's 41 electoral votes marked the end of Ford's presidency.

---

* The 1960 election's exact total of popular votes is murky because Democrats in Alabama voted for an unusual 11-man slate of 5 pro-Kennedy electors and 6 unpledged, pro-segregation electors, and which electors each voter actually preferred is impossible to know. The Kennedy electors in Alabama received 34% more votes than the Nixon electors, however, and the unpledged electors had sometimes hinted that they might vote for Kennedy. So most observers have concluded that Kennedy won Alabama's popular vote, even though six weeks later the state's six pro-segregation electors cast their electoral votes for Senator Harry Byrd of Virginia.

Why We Have Winner-Take-All

The two-extra-votes-per-state distortion that benefits the rural states is a part of Article II of the Constitution, but the winner-take-all system that helps the urban states began in Virginia in 1800 as a response by Virginia's state legislature to some odd features of the elections of 1788 and 1796.

In the autumn of 1788, a problem with having the state legislatures choose presidential electors arose in New York. (New York had finally ratified the Constitution in July of that year only after Alexander Hamilton warned upstate leaders that New York City and Long Island were prepared to secede from the state to join the newly formed United States, and if necessary, leave upstate New York on its own.)* In the 1788 election, every member of New York's state senate and state assembly supported George Washington for president, but the two houses could not agree on who the electors should be and failed to reach a compromise. As a result, New York did not cast any electoral votes for president in 1788, and this fiasco helped persuade legislators in other states that in the future it would be better to let the people vote for president.

Eight years later, when John Adams narrowly defeated Thomas Jefferson in 1796, only half of the nation's state legislatures still picked their state's presidential electors. In the other half of the states, the people chose their presidential electors, often by means of direct elections for individual electors held in special electoral districts. In 1796 the northern states, except for evenly divided Pennsylvania, awarded all of their electoral votes to Adams, while the southern states cast their electoral votes for Jefferson. But in Virginia and North Carolina, although the overwhelming majority of the people supported Jefferson, Adams managed to win one electoral vote in each state (out of the two states' 33 electoral districts), and it was those two votes that gave Adams his margin of victory, because the nation's final total was 71 electoral votes for Adams and 68 votes for Jefferson.

---

* Virginia also ratified the Constitution in time to vote for president in 1788, over the strong objection of Patrick Henry, who thought the new federal government was much too powerful. Henry denounced the coming "tyranny of Philadelphia" and warned his fellow Virginians, "They'll free your niggers."

Had Virginia and North Carolina chosen their electors on a state-wide basis rather than by individual districts, the two extra votes that Adams won would have been cast for Jefferson instead, and the national tally would have been 70 electoral votes for Jefferson and 69 for Adams. Jefferson would have become the nation's second president and Adams the vice president, not the other way around.

James Madison, Jefferson's close friend and ally, was determined never to let maverick districts determine an election's outcome again. Three years later, when the election of 1800 approached, Madison asked Virginia's legislature to change the state's election law so that in the future the legislature would pick a single, statewide slate of electors. But Virginia's legislators, having already granted the people the power to choose presidential electors directly, were reluctant to take that power away. Instead, they passed a new law in January 1800 that continued to have the people vote for electors directly, but reorganized the contest to be winner-take-all: From now on there would be just one statewide vote for *all* of the electors. Never again would John Adams or any other Federalist be able to win a stray southern elector by finishing first in a swing district.

In Massachusetts the people had also voted for individual presidential electors in special electoral districts, but the Bay State's legislators, who were Federalists, wanted to prevent Jefferson from picking up a stray elector in one of their swing districts, so they followed Virginia's lead and made Massachusetts a winner-take-all state too.

By 1804 six states were choosing presidential electors on a winner-take-all basis. The winner-take-all system maximized a state party's national influence, and once a few states adopted this arrangement, the other states had to follow to keep from losing their share of power. Any other method of awarding electoral votes would have been like unilateral disarmament. Pennsylvania, for example, had a much greater influence on the presidential election of 1796, when all 15 of its electors were united behind John Adams, than it did in 1800, when its electors were split 8 to 7 between Jefferson and Adams.

Thomas Jefferson was deeply troubled by the winner-take-all system, but even he conceded that it was "worse than folly" for the rest of the states not to adopt the format. By 1836 every state was using the winner-take-all format except South Carolina, where the legislature continued to chose the state's electors until 1868.

Today, changing the winner-take-all system would not require a constitutional amendment, only state legislation. But there is no incentive for the populous urban states to give up the extra power that the winner-take-all system gives them unless the rural states also agreed to reduce the two-extra-electors-per-state distortion, and, unfortunately, this distortion is entrenched in our Constitution. So any kind of national compromise between the urban states and rural states to change both the winner-take-all system's magnification effect and Article II's two-extra-votes-per-state distortion will require a constitutional amendment.

DEADLOCKS ARE DECIDED BY THE HOUSE OF REPRESENTATIVES

America's electoral system has thwarted the will of the people and given us runner-up presidents in 1876, 1888, and 2000. But for better or worse, it also makes things difficult for third parties. No matter how constructive a role a third-party candidate might play in a national election, he or she cannot win a single electoral vote by finishing third, or even second, in a state's popular vote. It is first or bust, and year after year this forces Americans to vote for candidates from one of the two major parties in order not to "throw their vote away."

By making the two-party system stable, the winner-take-all system has prevented a repeat of 1824's four-candidate election, when no one won a majority of the electoral vote and the election therefore moved to the House of Representatives.

Under Article II (and Amendments XII and XX) of the Constitution, if no candidate has won a majority of the electoral vote, the incoming House of Representatives chooses the president from among the three top electoral-vote winners, *with each state, large and small, having one vote.* For example, Wyoming's single congresswoman would have a vote equal to that of all 53 of California's congressmen and congresswomen. This is not only unfair, it's absurd.

In 1825, the last time this happened, the votes of the four "lone" congressmen (from Delaware and from the new states of Illinois, Mississippi, and Missouri) were equal to those of the 94 congressmen from New York, Pennsylvania, Massachusetts, and Virginia.

When all the congressmen from the nation's 24 states finally voted on February 9, John Quincy Adams won the votes of 13 states and became America's sixth president. Andrew Jackson had won 41% of the popular vote, however, while Adams had won only 31%. Jackson's supporters felt cheated and angry, and in Congress they prevented Adams from accomplishing much as president.

—◦—

If an election were thrown to the House of Representatives today, the voting would be even more unfair now than it was back then. When the Constitution was written in 1787, the largest state, Virginia, had 13 times more people than the smallest state, Delaware. In the 21st century, California has *70* times as many people as the least populous state, Wyoming.

Today, the seven representatives from the seven states with the fewest people (Wyoming, Vermont, North Dakota, Alaska, South Dakota, Delaware, and Montana) would have a voting power equal to the *195* House members from the seven states with the most people (California, Texas, Florida, New York, Illinois, Pennsylvania, and Ohio). And if a state's congressmen and congresswomen should happen to be evenly divided (if, for example, Ohio's 16 House members were split 8 to 8), then because no candidate had won a majority of the divided delegation, the state would be unable to cast a vote for president in the House at all.

If the House of Representatives decided a presidential election today, a candidate would need the votes of a majority (26) of the 50 states to win, which in a three-candidate race could be difficult, especially if some of the delegations were evenly split and therefore not voting. The temptation for congressmen to make secret deals to try to build a majority would be enormous, and the final result might seem tainted.

Another strange provision in Article II of the Constitution says that if no vice presidential candidate wins a majority of the electoral vote, the Senate, not the House of Representatives, shall choose the vice president. (Oddly enough, this did not happen in the winter of 1824–25 because Andrew Jackson and John Quincy Adams both had the same running mate: John Calhoun of South Carolina.) Thus if each house of Congress were controlled by opposing political parties, as is often the case, the vice president chosen by the Senate could easily come from a different political party than the president picked by the House, which might encourage a would-be assassin. And if no presidential candidate had won the support of at least 26 of the state delegations in the House of Representatives by Inauguration Day (January 20), then the vice president chosen by the Senate would serve as acting president until the House could resolve its deadlock.

WHAT WERE THE FOUNDING FATHERS THINKING?

Why did the Framers make the balloting in the House of Representatives one-state-one-vote? For that matter, how did we get electoral votes in the first place?

When the Founding Fathers wrote the Constitution in 1787, they had no idea that presidential candidates would soon be waging national campaigns. They thought that after George Washington died or retired, no one would ever win a majority of the nation's electoral votes again. The Framers assumed that the state-by-state casting of electoral votes would just be a nominating process, with the House of Representatives making the final choice for president from among the candidates who won the most electoral votes, although this has happened only twice, after the 1800 and 1824 elections.

Many of the Founders thought that the House of Representatives should choose the president because its members were popularly elected, and because they did not want the Senate to have the power both to elect and impeach a chief executive. But others thought the states should pick the president through their agents in the Senate.

Connecticut's Roger Sherman (the grandfather of General William Tecumseh Sherman), a self-educated son of a shoemaker who not only practiced law, but published a book of poetry, an almanac of astronomical observations, and an essay on monetary theory, proposed a compromise: If no one received a majority of the electoral vote, the House of Representatives would choose the president, but do it on a one-state-one-vote basis. This method appealed to the small states because the votes of Delaware, New

Hampshire, and Rhode Island would be equal to those of New York, Pennsylvania, and Virginia, and because the Senate, which was also weighted in favor of the small states, would pick the vice president separately.

The Founders endorsed Sherman's peculiar procedure almost unanimously not so much because of its merit, but because they were tired after four months of hours-long political discussions. The Constitutional Convention had begun on May 25, 1787, because the feeble government created by the Articles of Confederation had no money, no income, and only 700 soldiers. Confidence in America's economy was so low that in Amsterdam, American bonds traded for less than one-third of their face value. In the face of these difficulties, Benjamin Franklin urged his fellow delegates to put aside their local interests and compromise, so that America's government could be something designed "by human wisdom and [not left] to chance, war and conquest."

During most of the convention, the delegates found it uncomfortable to talk about the presidency of their future government with George Washington in the room, knowing full well that he would be America's first chief executive. Washington had been elected president of the Constitutional Convention unanimously and lent the assembly great prestige, but he almost didn't attend because a group of Revolutionary War veterans, the Society of Cincinnati, was also meeting in Philadelphia that summer. Washington disapproved of the society because its members had made their enrollment hereditary, and the general did not want to attend one convention in Philadelphia and snub the other. But James Madison and Alexander Hamilton refused to take "no" for an answer, and asked Washington again and again to attend the convention until at last the great general agreed to come.

With Washington silent but present at the convention every day, two months passed before the rest of the delegates finally had the courage to talk about how to elect a president. For 10 days in late July, they thought about having Congress elect a president every four years, but this seemed to make the president too subservient to the legislature. The Framers also considered a 7-year term, an 11-year term, and even a 15-year term. When Rufus King of Massachusetts stood up and mockingly shouted "Twenty years!" as if the proceeding were an auction, everyone laughed, but then

King added, "This is the median life of princes." At this point nearly all the delegates agreed that a long presidential term was too much like monarchy.

The Founders also thought about allowing the people to vote for president directly, but ultimately decided that this would hurt not just the small states but the southern states as well, because they had fewer white people, and therefore fewer voters, than the northern states did. Two proposals for a direct vote for president were defeated by the lopsided votes of 10 states to 1, and 9 states to 2. (There were never more than 11 state's delegations present at the Constitutional Convention at any one time.)

Afterward, Pennsylvania's James Wilson suggested that a president could be independent of the legislature if congressmen drew 15 of their names from a hat, let these legislators vote for president, and then immediately disbanded. The Framers rejected this proposal too, but Wilson's idea that a *temporary* group of electors should choose the president ultimately proved persuasive.

Meanwhile, it was hot in Philadelphia, even in the morning. Wire screens had not yet been invented, so every day the Founders faced an unhappy choice: either open the windows of Pennsylvania's State House, where the Declaration of Independence had been signed 11 years earlier, and suffer a plague of flies and mosquitoes, or close the windows and endure stifling heat.

On August 31, 1787, after weeks of discussions and no major decisions, the delegates decided to move things along and formed what they candidly called a Committee of Postponed Parts. The committee, with 10 unusually able men from 10 different states, was a kind of constitutional convention in miniature, without the long speeches that one delegate complained were "full of disputation and noisy as the wind." Chaired by New Jersey's David Brearly, the new group included James Madison, Roger Sherman, Gouverneur Morris, and Delaware's John Dickinson.

After four days the committee initially decided that Congress should elect the president to a four-year term. Their work seemed done, but then John Dickinson, who had been sick and arrived late to a meeting, begged his colleagues to reconsider. America's Commander in Chief, he said, should be "a man of the people," not a puppet of a faction-filled legislature.

Bronx-born Gouverneur Morris agreed. (Three neighborhoods in the New York City borough, Morris Heights, Morrisania, and Morris Park, are named for his land-owning family.) Just a few weeks earlier, Morris had also wanted the people to elect the president directly, and warned, "If the legislature elects [the president], it will be the work of intrigue, of cabal, and of faction: it will be like the election of a pope by a conclave of cardinals; real merit will rarely be the title to the appointment." Now Morris, who in spite of his peg leg (which came from jumping out of a lover's second-story window to avoid a husband who had come home early) was universally admired for his cheerful manner, impish wit, and continued success with women, suggested softly, "Come Gentleman, let us sit down again, and converse further."*

In response to Morris's plea, James Madison picked up a pen and began to outline the electoral system that we still use today. Madison, who was only five-feet-five-inches tall and too frail to have served in the Revolutionary War, was unassuming and straitlaced by day, but at dinner loved to hear, and tell, funny and sometimes racy jokes and stories. At the Constitutional Convention, however, Madison commanded enormous respect because he knew more than anyone else there about British and American law, and about the lessons to be learned from the rise and fall of previous democracies in Athens, Rome, the Netherlands, and Venice. Keenly aware of how few written records there were from antiquity, Madison decided to take detailed notes of the convention's daily sessions, which were closed both to journalists and to the public. Alone among the 55 delegates, he attended the convention nearly every hour of every day.†

---

* Only days later, James Madison and Alexander Hamilton asked Gouverneur Morris to rewrite the Constitution to improve its style. Morris reduced the number of articles in the Constitution from 23 to 7 and wrote the Preamble that begins, "We the People of the United States, in Order to form a more perfect Union . . ."

A month or two earlier, in a famous bet, Hamilton had dared Morris to slap George Washington on the back in friendship, promising to buy Morris dinner if he did. Morris took the dare, and during the backslap said, "My dear General, how happy I am to see you look so well." But the look that Washington gave him was so withering that Morris told Hamilton he would not slap the general again for a thousand dinners.

† Only about 30 men attended the Constitutional Convention on any given day. Delegates felt free to arrive late, leave early, and leave for weeks at a time to take care of their own farms and businesses. Of the 42 delegates who were still in Philadelphia when the convention ended on September 17, 1787, 39 of them signed the final document, then walked together to the City Tavern for a farewell dinner.

Similarities to the Roman Republic

Madison, who could read Latin as well as Greek, Hebrew, and French, was clearly influenced by the Roman Republic when he created the American electoral system, because ancient Roman and modern American elections have some remarkable similarities.

During the five centuries of the Roman Republic (509–27 BCE), citizens belonged to four urban districts and up to 31 rural districts. Election Day, which usually included gladiatorial contests, typically fell in late July, but sometimes officials could postpone it for a day or two if they saw bad omens such as lightning and thunder. Men arrived in Rome from all over Italy to cast their votes in a large field nicknamed the "sheep pen" because it had 35 roped-in lanes, each of which were hundreds of yards long. For more than 350 years the Romans voted orally, but after 139 BCE they wrote the initials of the candidate they favored on wooden tablets and tossed them into baskets.

If the Roman Republic had held direct, one-man-one-vote elections, citizens in the city of Rome's four districts would have consistently outvoted everyone from the other 31 districts farther away. Voting was therefore by district, not by individual, and each of Italy's 35 districts had one equal vote. Even though thousands of men in Rome cast ballots while only a few citizens arrived to vote from Sicily, each district still had an equal weight, just as our states have a specified number of electoral votes no matter how big or small the voter turnout in each state might ultimately be.

Similarly, if one Roman district's support for a leader was overwhelming while in another district the voters were closely divided, the votes of the two districts were still counted equally, just as in 2012 Barack Obama took Massachusetts's 11 electoral votes after receiving 61% of the votes there, while Mitt Romney took Arizona's 11 electoral votes despite winning only 53% of that state's voters.

Another striking parallel between the Roman Republic and the United States is that a Roman candidate needed the votes of a majority of Italy's districts to win office, just as an American candidate for president needs a majority of the nation's 538 electoral votes (i.e., 270) to win the presidency. Within a Roman district, however, a candidate did not need a majority of the votes in the district to win; it was sufficient if he just had more votes there than anyone else. Similarly, an American presidential candidate today does not need to win a majority of a state's popular vote to win that state's electoral votes; it is enough if he or she simply has more votes than anyone else in the state.

The Roman system of voting greatly favored rich men who could afford to travel to Rome from distant provinces, a bias Madison was surely aware of, but the vote count itself was honest because officials swore an oath to conduct the elections fairly. In a Roman election, however, because the popular vote was irrelevant, it was never recorded.

The Electoral Compromise

On September 4, 1787, the Committee of Postponed Parts recommended that "electors" chosen by the states should select the president, with each state's legislature free to decide for itself how their electors would be chosen. The number of electors a state would choose would be equal to the number of senators and representatives that the state had in Congress. Electoral votes were thus a compromise between the large states and small states, much like the earlier great compromise that had apportioned the House of Representatives according to population, while in the Senate the votes of the states were equal.

The electors would meet in their own state capitals, which would make a national conspiracy difficult. And the candidate who received the second-highest number of electoral votes would serve as vice president, a new office that the Founders had just created to make an unexpected presidential succession smooth. Until the 12th Amendment was ratified in 1804, each elector cast *two* votes for president, one of which had to be for a candidate from outside the elector's home state. (Casting two votes per person for president seemed like a good idea in 1787, but in 1800 it led to a dangerous constitutional crisis.)

Because both the small states and the southern states opposed the direct election of a president, Madison regarded the electoral system as the best substitute. Other delegates agreed that it was an ingenious improvement over prior proposals. If, for example, Congress had elected the president, many of the Founders believed that it would have blurred the separation of powers.

The "college" of presidential electors would be a short-lived group, unconnected to any legislature. As Alexander Hamilton would soon write in Federalist [Paper] No. 68, the Framers had "not made the appointment of the president to depend on pre-existing bodies of men, who might be tampered with beforehand to prostitute their votes." Instead, Hamilton wrote with approval, the electors would convene only "for the temporary and sole purpose of making the [presidential] appointment."

Once the Committee of Postponed Parts decided that electors should choose the president rather than Congress, the convention's delegates were no longer afraid that a future president might pander to congressional factions to stay in office. Because a president could now be reelected honorably, a shorter, four-year term with the possibility of reelection seemed to be a better alternative than a single, longer term of seven years.

On September 7, 1787, the Founders endorsed the new electoral system and the four-year presidential term. But because they continued to suffer from insects and humidity, they also quickly voted for Roger Sherman's one-state-one-vote compromise on how the House of Representatives would vote for president in case of an electoral deadlock. James Madison admitted that the Constitutional Convention "was not exempt from a degree of the hurrying influence produced by fatigue and impatience." Yet in the following year, during an otherwise heated national debate over whether the states should ratify the Constitution, hardly anyone in the 13 states criticized the new system of electoral votes, or how the House would vote in the event of a deadlock.

In the end, the kind of presidential election that the Framers envisioned— with the states choosing independent-minded electors to nominate candidates, and the House of Representatives voting state-by-state to pick a president from among these nominees—never came to be.

As early as 1796, when John Adams ran for president against Thomas Jefferson, only a handful of electors were still independent because nearly all of them had pledged to support one candidate or the other. By 1832, when Andrew Jackson ran for reelection, political parties nominated their presidential candidates at national conventions held months before the general election, and presidential electors, chosen for their loyalty, merely cast party-line votes.

Not everyone approved of the new party conventions. "I find these assemblies dangerous," John Quincy Adams told French author Alexis de Tocqueville, because "they usurp the place of [elected] political bodies." De Tocqueville agreed that mass-meetings could be dangerous, but also understood that at these conventions, "opinions are maintained with a warmth and energy that written language can never attain."

Since 1828 one major party's candidate or the other has always won a majority of the electoral vote despite the Founders' original assumption that no one after George Washington would ever be able to do so. This is because the winner-take-all system makes it hard for third parties to win any electoral votes at all. Even in the six elections when a third-party candidate won 10% or more of the popular vote (1856, 1860, 1912, 1924, 1968, and 1992), the winner-take-all system's "magnifying effect" has deprived third-party candidates of any real share of the electoral vote, and instead has always given the popular-vote winners (Buchanan, Lincoln, Wilson, Coolidge, Nixon, and Clinton) many more electoral votes than their shares of the popular vote warranted.

The winner-take-all system, because it weakens third parties and prevents electoral deadlocks, has kept elections from being decided by the House of Representatives. This is a huge benefit worth preserving. As unfair as it is for one candidate to take all of a state's electoral votes, changing the winner-take-all system is risky. We have to be careful that any reform that would reduce the chance of another runner-up presidency would not also increase the danger of an electoral deadlock, because a deadlock would lead to a one-state-one-vote circus in the House of Representatives.

THE DIFFICULTY OF CHANGING THE ELECTORAL SYSTEM

Constitutional amendments are rare. In the 225 years since the Bill of Rights was passed, only 17 additional amendments have been ratified. Passing an amendment requires three extremely difficult steps: a two-thirds vote in the House of Representatives, a two-thirds vote in the Senate, and ratification by three-fourths (38) of the 50 state legislatures.

This means the legislatures of the 13 least populous states can block an amendment even if all 37 of the larger states' legislatures have ratified it. In practice, an amendment usually passes only if big states, small states, and both major parties approve of the reform.

Senators and representatives have proposed *hundreds* of amendments to change America's electoral system over the last two centuries, but only one has passed: the 12th Amendment, ratified in 1804. It provides that electors must vote for a president and vice president separately.

The last time a proposal to change the electoral system even came to a vote in the House of Representatives was in 1969. The year before, a pro-segregation candidate, Governor George Wallace of Alabama, had won five states and 46 electoral votes, reviving the fear that an electoral deadlock could throw an election to the House of Representatives. In 1969 President Nixon supported a constitutional amendment to replace electoral votes with direct elections, and it passed the House by a lopsided vote, 339 to 70. According to a survey at the time by the Congressional Quarterly, a majority of the state senators and representatives in 44 of the nation's 50 state legislatures also favored direct elections.

But in the US Senate, a coalition of southern and small-state senators were worried that direct presidential elections would be dominated by the big northern cities, so they filibustered the bill and kept the Senate from even voting on the measure. Fifty-four senators favored direct elections, but it was not enough to end the filibuster and, in any case, it was well short of the 67 votes in the Senate needed to pass a constitutional amendment.

The 1969 bill was the first time that a call for direct elections had reached the floor of the House since 1826, and no such proposal has ever reached the House floor again, even though polls in decade after decade have consistently shown that two-thirds of Americans would prefer direct elections to the present electoral-vote system.

In 1979 another proposal for direct presidential elections was introduced in the Senate. It had the support of President Jimmy Carter, Kansas Senator Bob Dole, and both the AFL-CIO and the US Chamber of Commerce. But this time liberal senators such as Joe Biden of Delaware and Daniel Moynihan of New York opposed the reform, along with civil rights leaders such as Vernon Jordan, the president of the National Urban League. They were afraid that direct elections would reduce the power that Blacks, Jews, and other minorities enjoy as coveted voters in the urban states that have the most electoral votes. The Senate voted in favor of direct elections, 51 to 48, but it was far short of the two-thirds vote necessary to amend the Constitution, so the House of Representatives never even considered the measure. More ominously for the prospect of future reform, fully two-thirds of the 20 senators from the 10 smallest states voted against direct elections.

That both small-state conservatives and big-city liberals have successfully blocked any change to the electoral system shows just how incredibly difficult the task of reform is. Can the electoral system really benefit both groups? Yes. Small states benefit by having two more electoral votes than a state's population alone warrants, and big states benefit from the winner-take-all format. After two centuries, conservatives and liberals have both grown accustomed to the electoral system's oddities, but the fact that we are comfortable with our electoral system does not make it any less dangerous.

When Orrin Hatch, Utah's conservative Republican senator, helped defeat the proposal for direct elections in 1979, he defended America's electoral system as "a proven method of election that has adapted to every change and development in the political history of this country." Similarly, Daniel Moynihan, New York's liberal Democratic senator, said that abolishing the electoral system would be "the most radical transformation in our political system that has ever been considered," and warned his colleagues that eliminating it would lead to smaller and more extreme political parties, and possibly even to "the end of liberty." With such intense and widespread opposition to constitutional change, it is not surprising that no proposal to reform the electoral system has reached the floor of either house of Congress again for more than 35 years.

CHAPTER 2

Florida, *Bush v. Gore*, and the 2000 Election

ON ELECTION NIGHT 2000, THE NEWS NETWORKS, TO THE DELIGHT OF Democrats, initially called Florida, the biggest swing state, for Vice President Al Gore. Then they took back their call, and soon, to the delight of Republicans, called Florida for Texas Governor George W. Bush instead. Then the networks retracted their second call as the vote-counting continued all night. Finally, after five weeks, the US Supreme Court awarded Florida to Bush a final time. On the national election map, Florida was white, blue, white again, red, white a third time, and finally and permanently, red.

Officially, Bush won Florida by 537 votes out of almost 6 million cast:

George W. Bush	*2,912,790*
Al Gore	*2,912,253*
Ralph Nader	*97,488*
Patrick Buchanan	*17,484*
Harry Browne (Libertarian)	*16,415*

But as everyone knows, many votes in Florida were never counted because the manual recounts ordered by Florida's Supreme Court were stopped by the US Supreme Court. As a result, we do not even know how many people voted in Florida in 2000, much less the exact totals for Bush and Gore.

IF FLORIDA'S OFFICIALS HAD COUNTED EVERY VOTE, WHO WOULD HAVE WON?
Al Gore, but only by a hair. Statistically, the election was a tie.

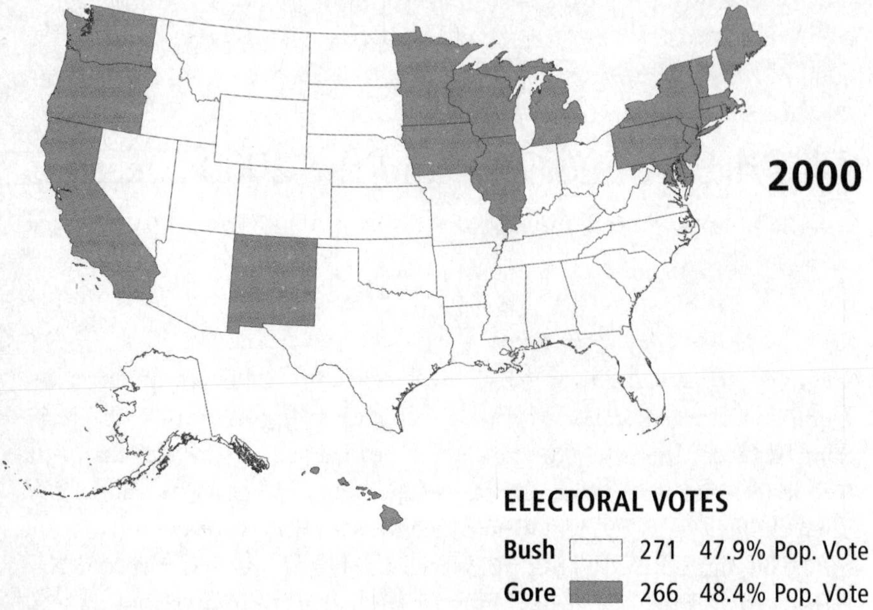
2000
ELECTORAL VOTES
Bush 271 47.9% Pop. Vote
Gore 266 48.4% Pop. Vote

The *Miami Herald*, *USA Today*, and several other newspapers looked at 64,248 punch card ballots on which no vote for president was recorded. Surprisingly, they found that when they used a lenient standard, counting every ballot that had a pinprick or a hanging rectangular "chad," George W. Bush won Florida by 1,665 votes. By contrast, when they applied a stricter standard that required three corners of a chad to be detached from a ballot to be counted, Gore won by three votes.

But hundreds of punch card ballots had disappeared by the time these newspapers made their count, and their study did not include any ballots from Palm Beach County, Broward County, or the northern part of Miami-Dade County, all strongly Democratic areas. When the same newspapers made a larger count later of 176,000 disputed ballots, they found that under the lenient standard, Gore won Florida by 393 votes, while under the strict standard Bush won the state by 97 votes.

Unfortunately, in November 2000 there was never a sustained attempt to count Florida's votes accurately. At the office where

Miami-Dade County was holding its recount, during what Paul Gigot, a columnist for the *Wall Street Journal*, called a "bourgeois riot," young Republicans banged on doors and windows, shouting "Shut the recount down!" and turned the building's heat up full-blast. They also told the three elderly officials in charge of Miami-Dade's recount that 1,000 angry Cuban-Americans were on their way to confront them, and this led the county commissioners to stop counting Miami-Dade's votes altogether.

In Palm Beach County, a grueling eight-day recount caused Gore to pick up 215 votes, cutting Bush's statewide lead by 40%. The Democratic officials in Palm Beach County followed a strict standard, counting a ballot only if a punched card's rectangular chad or chads were either dangling or had three dimples, because three dimples showed a pattern on the part of a voter while one or two dimples might simply have been random. By contrast, the Democratic officials in Broward County (Fort Lauderdale) counted dimples even if they were merely *near* a rectangular chad, a lax standard that understandably alarmed the Republicans.

Katherine Harris, who incredibly was both Florida's secretary of state (the state's top election official) and cochair of Bush's Florida campaign, refused to accept any part of Palm Beach County's careful recount, even though it was 99% complete, because the count was not finished until two hours after her firm but unnecessary 5:00 p.m. dead-line on November 26.

Two weeks later, on December 9, the US Supreme Court stopped all of the recounts that the Florida Supreme Court had previously authorized, then ruled three days later that the time for recounts had run out because Florida's electoral votes had to be certified at the beginning rather than at the end of the weeklong time period that the US Code provides for certification.

───

People can argue over how many of Florida's votes should have been recounted by hand, and what standards the election officials who were doing the counting should have used. What is less well-known but far more disturbing is that 18 of Florida's 67 counties, representing one-fourth of the state's population, never even performed the mandatory *machine* recounts that Florida law requires when an election is close. (Secretary of State Katherine Harris knew about this omission, but did nothing about it.)

Months later the *Orlando Sentinel* determined that if Lake County, just west of Orlando, had performed a recount using the strictest standards of determining voter intent, 622 previously uncounted ballots would have subsequently been counted. On 376 of these ballots, voters filled in an oval for Al Gore and also wrote in his name, while on 246 ballots voters filled in an oval for George Bush and wrote in Bush's name. Machines discarded all of these ballots as double-votes even though the intent of the voters could not have been clearer. So even with the strictest standard of determining voter intent, a proper recount would have produced a net gain for Gore in Lake County of 130 votes (376 minus 246). Bush's official statewide lead would have fallen from 537 votes to 407, and this reduction would have come from just one of Florida's 67 counties.

Across the state, Florida's voting machines threw out 180,110 ballots—2.93% of the statewide vote in 2000, up from 2.52% in 1996—partly because about 15% of the Blacks who voted in Florida in 2000 had never cast a ballot before, and many of these new voters did not know how to cast one properly. In Jacksonville, for example, more than 40% of the almost 27,000 votes discarded came from just four Black-majority precincts, and in two Black-majority precincts near Palm Beach, the proportion of ballots thrown out for oval-plus-write-in double-voting was more than 15% of the total.

Punch card ballots—which had a 4% chance of not being counted by a machine because a clumsy, confused, or inexperienced voter might fail to punch a rectangular chad all the way through—were more common in Florida's poorer districts. By contrast, optical scan ballots—which had only a 0.7% chance of not being counted by a machine because all a voter had to do was fill in an oval—were more common in affluent areas. Across Florida, more than 180,000 ballots were spoiled, defective, or simply missed by a machine, and these uncounted ballots were four times more prevalent in Black-majority precincts than in white-majority ones.

For poorly educated voters, punch card ballots became an unintentional literacy test.

—◆—

Florida's final vote total can be disputed, but the preference of the majority of Florida's voters for Gore was clear. The election became close because of Palm Beach County's infamous two-page "butterfly" ballot, which flummoxed thousands of mostly elderly voters. The confusing ballot caused them to either mistakenly vote twice, thinking that they were also voting for a vice presidential candidate, or inadvertently vote for the ultraconservative candidate, Patrick Buchanan, whose "hole" for punching was located in between Bush's and Gore's. Even Buchanan has cheerfully conceded that he could never have won the more than 7,000 votes he received in liberal and heavily Jewish Palm Beach County if the butterfly ballot had not been so confusing.

Throughout Palm Beach County, 5,530 voters spoiled their ballots by punching holes for both Gore and Buchanan, 1,631 voters ruined their votes by punching holes for both Bush and Buchanan, and 2,908 voters punched holes for both Gore and a Socialist, David McReynolds, because McReynolds's hole was just below Gore's and therefore seemed as if it might have been a hole for Gore's running mate, Joe Lieberman. Altogether, 4.16% of the voters in Palm Beach County spoiled their ballots by voting twice, up from 0.75% in 1996. The net loss for Gore was 6,607 votes, which was 10 times more than enough for him to have won both Florida and the presidency.

WHY DID THE US SUPREME COURT STOP FLORIDA'S RECOUNT?

On December 12, 2000, the US Supreme Court, by a 5-to-4 majority, said Florida's recount was unconstitutional because the different standards used from one county to another as to which ballots were valid and which ballots were invalid violated the Equal Protection Clause of the 14th Amendment, which says that no state shall "deny to any person within its jurisdiction the equal protection of the laws."

Florida law says that a precinct must count a ballot if a voter's intention is clear, and expressly authorizes manual recounts. But during the recounts in 2000, the standards for determining a voter's intent varied from county to county. In Broward County (Fort Lauderdale), a dimple that was merely near a punch card's chad was considered enough to show a voter's intent, while in Palm Beach County chads had to be "dangling," with at least two of a chad's four corners separated from the punch card.

In *Breaking the Deadlock*, a thoughtful book on the 2000 election, Federal Judge Richard Posner (a Republican) analyzed the difficulties involved when government officials try to gauge a voter's intent. "Republicans were entitled to be concerned about hand recounts by canvassing boards dominated by Democrats," Posner said, pointing out that "like the census, an election is a count, not a statistical projection." Election officials and judges were therefore right to refuse "to classify an error by the voter as an error in the tabulation."

With similar logic, the US Supreme Court not only ruled that the Florida's counties' "recount mechanisms . . . do not satisfy the minimum requirement for non-arbitrary treatment of voters," it also said that the time to do anything about the differing standards of recounts from county to county had run out. The time to recount Florida's votes in 2000 had expired because the week of December 12–18, the nation's deadline for choosing presidential electors, had arrived.

In fact, there could have been at least six more days (until December 18) for Florida's Supreme Court to standardize the state's recount and for county election boards to count more votes. Under a law passed in 1887 (when the frightening uncertainty of the disputed 1876 election was fresh) that is still in force today, Congress codified presidential election procedure. The law says that the day that electors must meet in their respective state capitals to vote for president and vice president is the first Monday after the second Wednesday in December, which in 2000 was December 18. But another part of the same law says that if a state finishes picking its presidential electors six days or more before the electors actually meet, the state's choice of its electors shall be safe from any later challenge in Congress.

Although no Florida law or court decision ever said that Florida's deadline for choosing its electors had to be December 12 rather than December 18, the US Supreme Court cited one line from a Florida

Supreme Court decision on December 8 that said that the state's electors should "participate fully in the federal electoral process," and used this phrase to hold that Florida's deadline for choosing its electors had to be December 12, despite the fact that Florida's Supreme Court had expressly ruled that it wanted the recount to continue. "That date is upon us," said the five US justices in the majority (William Rehnquist, Sandra Day O'Connor, Antonin Scalia, Anthony Kennedy, and Clarence Thomas) when December 12 arrived, so the Supreme Court's temporary halt to Florida's recount that the court had ordered three days before, on December 9, now became permanent—making George W. Bush the winner of the 2000 presidential election after five weeks of nail-biting.

~

One reason so many legal scholars, even conservatives, think the Supreme Court's reasoning in *Bush v. Gore* is unconvincing is that the court's remedy for the differing recount standards in Florida's 67 counties was not the obvious step of ordering Florida's counties to standardize their recounts, but instead to stop the recounts altogether, which meant that the more than 180,000 ballots across the state that the machines had missed would never be tallied. In other words, the Supreme Court's solution to Florida's equal protection difficulties was to create a much more serious equal protection problem.

Few conservative legal scholars believe that the Supreme Court would have ruled for Al Gore if the facts had been reversed and Gore had been ahead while trying to stop the recount. As for liberal scholars, most of them feel that the Supreme Court deprived Gore of the victory that a careful manual recount would have given him. Many of them agree with Harvard Law Professor Alan Dershowitz, who called *Bush v. Gore* "the single most corrupt decision in Supreme Court history," because justices who had never wanted to interfere with a state government's decisions, even when a condemned prisoner's life was at stake, suddenly ignored their own previous rulings on the importance of state autonomy in order to stop Florida's recount.

In the past, courts had always used the 14th Amendment's Equal Protection Clause to increase, not decrease, the number of voters—to make sure that Blacks and other disadvantaged minorities could vote. By contrast, the *Bush v. Gore* decision ensured that thousands of ballots by minority voters would never be counted.

The five justices in the US Supreme Court's majority openly admitted their lack of interest in the details of equal protection—the mechanics of voter registration, punch card ballots, and recount procedures—when they declared that their decision should not be seen as a precedent in future voting disputes. "Our consideration is limited to the present circumstances," they wrote in *Bush v. Gore*'s most infamous sentence, "for the problem of equal protection in election processes generally presents many complexities." The justices in the majority did not try to improve Florida's recount, or set any standards for the future. They just wanted to end it.

In fact, the three most conservative justices—William Rehnquist, Antonin Scalia, and Clarence Thomas—did not want to use any equal protection reasoning at first. They thought the Florida Supreme Court's supervision of the recount was a violation of Article II, Section 1, of the US Constitution, which gives state legislatures (and their hired officials) the sole authority over a state's choice of its presidential electors. But the three judges were a minority. The other six justices felt—as do most conservative scholars—that a state's supreme court has the right to interpret its own state laws, including election laws.

If the three most conservative judges had stuck to their original position, the final result of stopping Florida's recount would have been the same, but there would have been two opinions justifying the halt, and neither opinion would have had a majority. So with less than two days left to write a decision before the justices' self-imposed vote-counting deadline of December 12 arrived, the three most conservative judges agreed to concur with Sandra Day O'Connor's and Anthony Kennedy's reasoning that the different recount standards used from one county to the next violated the 14th Amendment's Equal Protection Clause.

Even conservative scholars are uncomfortable with the *Bush v. Gore* decision because federal courts usually let state courts interpret their own state's laws. But the Republicans on the US Supreme Court felt that the judges on Florida's Supreme Court, all Democrats, had usurped the authority of Florida's election officials, as granted to them by the state legislature, which under the US Constitution has the final say in determining the rules for choosing presidential electors.

Of course, if Florida's secretary of state, Katherine Harris had recused herself from the recount and had left the legal rulings to career election officials, or if she at least had been less one-sided in her conduct, Florida's Supreme Court might never have had to order a recount, because a recount might already have been under way.

The fact that the US Supreme Court accepted the case of *Bush v. Gore*, and took the unusual step of ruling on Florida's election law, suggests that for a majority of the judges, having a clear, quick, and final election result was more important than determining the intent of every last Florida voter. The justices did not trust a body as undisciplined as the US Congress to handle the disputed election competently in early January, with Inauguration Day just two weeks away. The chaos had to end.

WHAT IF THE RECOUNTS HAD CONTINUED?

What if the Supreme Court had not taken the case? If Governor George W. Bush had remained ahead, his election would have been assured. But what if Vice President Al Gore had pulled ahead? In 2000 the Republicans had a majority in both houses of Florida's legislature, and many of the legislators deeply distrusted the manual recounts in southern Florida's Democratic counties. Some state representatives warned that if the Democrats changed the election result, the legislators would take the power to choose Florida's presidential electors away from the state's voters and return it to the legislature, something that every state legislature has the right to do, although no legislature has done such a thing since the early 19th century. Florida's legislature could then have picked 25 Republican electors. But Title 3, Section 6, of the US Code says that states must choose their method of selecting presidential electors *before* the election, so the threats by Florida's Republican legislators to override the state's popular vote had little force.

If Florida's manual recounts had continued, however, it is possible that there would have been competing tallies. One set of numbers, certified by

Florida's Republican governor, Jeb Bush, might have said that George W. Bush won the most votes, while another tally, perhaps certified by the Florida Supreme Court's chief justice, Charles T. Wells, a Democrat, might have said that Al Gore won the most votes.

Under the US Election Law of 1887, if a state presents Congress with two or more competing certificates for electoral votes, the House and Senate must vote separately on which certificate to approve. If the House and Senate pick different certificates, the certificate signed by the state's governor shall control. Because in 2001 the US House of Representatives had a large Republican majority, it would have approved the certificate signed by Governor Jeb Bush no matter what the US Senate (which at the time was divided 50–50) decided. So a recount that showed Gore in the lead would not have had enough support in Congress to matter. A certificate signed by Governor Jeb Bush that his brother, George W. Bush, had won Florida's 25 electoral votes would probably have been sufficient to secure George Bush the presidency.

This is the messy prospect that the five conservative justices on the US Supreme Court most likely wanted to avoid. They may have known that their equal protection reasoning in *Bush v. Gore* was weak, but probably felt that the decision was a lesser evil than the chaos that would have followed had there been two competing recounts, another month of electoral uncertainty, and the probability of yet another Supreme Court case at a time when the constitutional crisis would have been even greater than before. And if the dispute over Florida's electoral votes had continued past Inauguration Day, January 20, then the Republican Speaker of the House, Dennis Hastert of Illinois, would have been sworn in as a temporary acting president until Congress—with the government of the United States in the balance—finally certified either Bush or Gore as president.

Still, whether the motives of the Supreme Court's justices were altruistic or political, the fact remains that the court appropriated the power to decide a disputed election, overriding not only Florida's courts and legislature, but also the authority of the US Congress.

WOULD GORE HAVE WON FLORIDA IF RALPH NADER HAD NOT RUN?

Yes, definitely. Ralph Nader won only 1.6% of the vote in Florida, well below his nationwide total of 2.7%, but it was more than enough to deprive Al Gore of victory.

Suppose that Nader, Patrick Buchanan, and Libertarian Harry Browne had not been on the ballot in Florida in 2000, and that every one of Florida's 33,899 supporters of Buchanan and Browne had voted for George W. Bush instead. Suppose further that half of Florida's 97,488 Nader voters would have stayed home rather than vote for Al Gore. If the other half of Nader's supporters had voted for Gore, Gore's statewide lead over Bush would have been 14,845 votes. This would have been more than enough to withstand recounts, and Gore would have won the presidency.

———

Nationally, Al Gore beat George W. Bush by nearly 544,000 popular votes in 2000, and Ralph Nader outpolled Patrick Buchanan by more than a 5-to-1 margin. A small but clear majority of Americans wanted a left-of-center government, yet because of our antiquated electoral system, that is not what they received.

Many conservatives are grateful that our 18th-century electoral system spared them from four (and possibly eight) years of a Gore presidency. But thoughtful conservatives know that the electoral system can just as easily swing from a pro-rural to a pro-urban bias, as in fact it did in 2012, when winner-take-all majorities in the northern swing states ensured that President Obama would have been reelected even if he had lost the popular vote to Mitt Romney by as many as 1.9 million votes.

CHAPTER 3

The Loser Wins

Rutherford B. Hayes (1876)

ALL FIVE OF THE PRESIDENTIAL ELECTIONS BETWEEN 1876 AND 1892 were unusually close, with one candidate always finishing within 3% of the popular vote of the other, and more often, within 1%. *Twice*, in 1876 and 1888, a candidate who received fewer popular votes than his opponent won the electoral vote and the presidency.

The man who won 51% of the popular vote in 1876 but still lost the election was the corruption-fighting Democratic governor of New York, Samuel Tilden, who won a national reputation by putting America's most dishonest politician, Boss Tweed, in jail. Short, frail, pallid, and a lifelong bachelor, Tilden was born in 1814 and grew up in New Lebanon, New York, a small town east of Albany on the stagecoach route to Boston. A reporter for the *New York Herald* interviewed Tilden's friends and neighbors and wrote:

> *No one remembered his robbing an apple orchard, or his running away from school to go swimming, or playing hooky to go fishing, horse racing, hiding his grandmother's spectacles or indulging in any other pastimes for which country boys are generally noted all over the land. He enjoyed his books and his studies, was a good mathematician, the marvel of his teachers.* *

---

* Roy Morris, *Fraud of the Century* (New York: Simon & Schuster, 2003), 136.

His father owned a general store and also sold patent medicines. Both father and son were hypochondriacs and constantly suffered colds, chills, fevers, stiffness, hoarseness, toothaches, insomnia, and stomach pains. While other boys fished, Tilden was often sick in bed, reading. As a teenager, he read Adam Smith's *The Wealth of Nations* and the letters of Thomas Jefferson. Tilden did enjoy riding horses in the foothills of the Berkshire Mountains, "but I always shrank," he said later, "from killing harmless birds and animals for sport."

Tilden's father, a local politician, was friends with Martin Van Buren, America's eighth president. Young Samuel wrote pamphlets and position papers on banking for Van Buren, who was a Democrat, in 1836, the year he was elected president, and again four years later, when Van Buren lost to William Henry Harrison.

Tilden briefly attended Yale, studying Latin, Greek, and mathematics, but left after less than a year because he could not stomach the food. He then went to law school at New York University and was admitted to the New York Bar in 1841. In 1843, thanks to recommendation letters from six judges, Tilden was appointed Corporation Counsel of the City of New York. He prosecuted minor offenses such as selling liquor or driving a horse-drawn cab on Sunday, keeping more hogs than was permitted by law, driving a carriage at more than five miles per hour, or dumping coal ash into the street. Later, in private practice, Tilden helped troubled railroads with mergers, acquisitions, and reorganizations. Wisely, he often took stock certificates as payment instead of money, and eventually was worth $6 million, or more than $100 million in today's money.

Tilden hated slavery, but in 1860 he supported the Democratic candidate for president, Stephen Douglas, because he was afraid that electing Lincoln as president would cause the South to secede. When seven states did secede following Lincoln's victory, Tilden opposed using force to bring them back into the Union, although once Southern troops fired on Fort Sumter, he actively supported the war. Tilden was too old for military service, but he sold the Union army, at cost, 6,000 tons of iron from mines that he co-owned in Upper Michigan, as well as the machines needed to cast the iron into guns.

In 1864 Tilden favored the Democratic candidate for president, former general George McClellan, and helped finance his campaign, although both he and McClellan were against the party's platform that called for an immediate ceasefire and peace negotiations with the South. McClellan saw the war as necessary to preserve the union, but said that once the Southern states rejoined the nation, they should enjoy their full prewar rights, which implied that freeing slaves was just a temporary measure during wartime. As for Tilden, although he had strongly opposed the Democratic Party's call for a negotiated peace, many Republicans regarded him as a Confederate-sympathizer for the rest of his life.

After the war, Tilden became chairman of New York's Democratic Party. He investigated the appalling corruption of New York City's William Marcy "Boss" Tweed, a flamboyant politician who wore loud checkered suits, diamond stickpins, and ruby cufflinks. With the slogan, "Something for Everyone," Tweed's machine, Tammany Hall, doubled the cost of city contracts by taking kickbacks worth more than $1 billion in today's money. Boss Tweed strengthened his power by paying Irish immigrants a dollar or two to "vote early and vote often." In one infamous sale, Tweed charged the city $180,000 (about $4 million in today's money) for three tables and 40 chairs. For a while, even New York's governor and mayor were on Tweed's payroll.

In 1871, with the help of one of Tweed's accountants, Tilden and the *New York Times* published a list of bribes, payoffs, and kickbacks with enough detail to put Tweed in prison on 120 counts of fraud, forgery, and grand larceny. Tweed escaped from jail and fled to Spain, but Tilden had him extradited and returned to prison, where Tweed finally died.

After grateful voters elected Tilden governor of New York in 1874, Tilden smashed upstate New York's crooked "Canal Ring," which was led, surprisingly, by a Presbyterian deacon. Because so many of the state's judges and legislators were on the take, the Canal Ring had received huge kickbacks from contractors who had tripled the cost of the Erie Canal's maintenance and repairs. Tilden hired an engineer who published 12 devastating reports that led to many indictments. Later, Tilden pushed and signed laws that made it a felony to use public money to pay false bills, as well as laws that made it easier to investigate, subpoena, and fire corrupt officials. He also reduced taxes and left a budget surplus.

Governor Tilden worked long hours, and often during dinner. "I can't help it," he said to his friends. "This work has to be done." He expected his subordinates to work equally hard, saying, "A man who is not single-minded is not worth a damn." Once, when a job applicant asked how many vacation days he would have, Tilden replied, "Your vacation will begin at once and will continue indefinitely."

1876

By 1876 Americans everywhere were tired of corruption, especially after the Grant administration's many scandals involving liquor taxes, steamship contracts, mining stock fraud, the bribing of customs officials, and Indian reservation graft. Recalling one of the mythic labors of Hercules, the *New York World* wished that "some [modern] Hercules" would come to Washington to "cleanse that Augean stable [just] as the city and state of New York are cleansing." To make Tilden's corruption-fighting record better known, supporters placed articles about Tilden's reforms in 1,200 newspapers across the country.

At the Democratic Convention in St. Louis, the delegates (not one of whom was Black) ignored warnings from New York City's boss-led delegates that Tilden would be an aloof and dull presidential candidate. The men at the convention wanted honesty, and gave Tilden 56% of their votes on the first ballot because he was a proven fighter for clean government. Until 1936, however, Democratic Party nominations required a two-thirds majority, so it took a second ballot before Tilden won the nomination. Tilden's vice presidential nominee was the presidential candidate who had won the second-most delegates, Indiana's Senator Thomas Hendricks, a bigot who had voted against the 13th Amendment that outlawed slavery.

The Republican who beat Samuel Tilden in 1876 with only 48% of the vote was the governor of Ohio, Rutherford Birchard Hayes, who became America's 19th president. A handsome red-haired war hero, "Rud" Hayes was born in 1822 and grew up in Delaware, Ohio, just north of Columbus. Both of his parents were originally from Vermont, but his father, a wealthy merchant, died before Hayes was born.

As a teenager, Hayes studied Latin, Greek, and mathematics before entering Kenyon College at 16. At the beginning and end of each school year, Hayes walked the 40 miles between home and college. He majored in both chemistry and philosophy, graduated first in his class, and then went to Harvard Law School. Hayes liked living in Boston and occasionally heard speeches by Daniel Webster and John Quincy Adams. By contrast, life was dull when he returned to Ohio to start a title-deed and debt-collection practice in Fremont, a town of only 1,000 people on the often icy Lake Erie.

In 1848 Hayes took a long vacation and traveled by steamboat to Galveston, Texas, to visit Guy Bryan, a classmate at Kenyon. (Bryan, Texas, a city of 70,000, is named for Guy's father.) During his visit, Hayes decided that slavery was not only bad for slaves, it was also bad for the character of their masters.

After his trip, Hayes moved to Cincinnati, where he quickly became known for defending fugitive slaves. He helped start the Cincinnati Literary Society, a group of young men who met weekly to debate issues, hear talks, and eat oysters. Hayes also helped launch Cincinnati's Republican Party, and in 1858 he became city solicitor after the previous solicitor was killed by a locomotive.

At 30, Hayes married 20-year-old Lucy Webb, a teetotaler from his hometown who began each day kneeling in prayer and ended each day singing a hymn. Years later, when she became America's first college-educated First Lady, she earned the nickname "Lemonade Lucy" because when she gave parties at the White House, guests joked, "the water flowed like wine."

Hayes met Abraham Lincoln briefly in 1859 and campaigned hard for him the following year. When the Civil War began, Hayes, 39, volunteered for duty even though he had three children, a pregnant wife, and an elderly mother. Like many men at the time, he was more afraid of missing the war than dying in it. The new recruits in Ohio's 23rd Regiment elected Hayes captain, and within six months, after helping to drive the

Confederates out of what is now West Virginia, he became a lieutenant colonel.

Hayes and his men enjoyed camping in the Shenandoah Mountains in the summer and fall. Writing his wife, he said, "We are a great grown-up armed blackberry party." Hayes added that he enjoyed living outdoors with his men "as much as a boy does the Fourth of July." By contrast, Ambrose Bierce, the author of *The Devil's Dictionary*, was also in West Virginia then and remembered seeing wild pigs eat the faces off dead soldiers.

Hayes fought in more than 50 battles, mostly in Virginia, and often led charges against enemy fire. He was wounded four times and almost died in western Maryland when a musket ball shattered a bone in his left arm three days before the Battle of Antietam. Hayes was operated on by his brother-in-law, who also served in the regiment, then spent the rest of 1862 at home with his family. He rejoined the army in 1863, and over the course of the war had four horses shot from under him. Once he was struck in the head by a bullet that had lost most of its force and simply bounced off him.

In the fall of 1864, Hayes helped General Philip Sheridan defeat the army of Confederate General Jubal Early, whose lightning-quick raids from the Shenandoah foothills briefly threatened Washington, DC. In Cincinnati, prominent Republicans asked Hayes to run for Congress. Disgusted by the offer, Hayes wrote, "An officer fit for duty who at this crisis would abandon his post and electioneer for a seat in Congress ought to be scalped." Cincinnati voters loved the quote and elected him anyway, and when the war ended in 1865, Hayes, by then a brigadier general, served his term in Congress.

In Washington, Hayes supported both the 14th Amendment, which gave Blacks equal protection under the law, as well as a new proposal that Blacks be given the right to vote. But these were controversial positions in Ohio. When Hayes ran for governor in 1867, he won by only ½ of 1% of the vote even though previous Republican candidates for the office had won by landslides.

As governor, Hayes improved the treatment of the mentally ill, helped start Ohio State University, and successfully pushed Ohio's legislature to ratify the 15th Amendment, which granted Blacks the right to vote. Hayes called the amendment a "triumph for justice and humanity," but in 1870 it passed the Ohio House of Representatives by only two votes and the Ohio Senate by only one. Then, as now, Ohio was a state evenly divided between the two major parties. When Hayes ran for a third term as governor in 1875, he again won by only a single percentage point.

Although Hayes was a third-term governor of the Midwest's most populous state, when the Republican Convention met in Cincinnati in 1876, only 8% of the delegates voted for him on the first ballot, and most of them were from Ohio. The front-runner for the presidential nomination that year was Maine's James G. Blaine, who had been Speaker of the US House of Representatives for six years until the Republicans lost control of the body to the Democrats in 1875. Blaine, a "magnetic man" who dressed stylishly and had a rich baritone voice, was a shoo-in for the nomination until the House Judiciary Committee discovered that an Arkansas railroad had given Blaine stock in return for his help with a federal grant of land to the railroad.

Technically it was legal because the gift of stock was only a sales commission, and when the railroad's stocks and bonds declined in value, Blaine merely broke even. Still, although Blaine's work for the railroad was neither criminal nor profitable, it smelled. As a delegate told one of Hayes's sons, "I hate like hell to vote for a man whose shirt tail is covered with shit." Suddenly Rutherford Hayes, a likable, scandal-free governor of an important state, became the second choice of many delegates.

To polite but weak applause, Frederick Douglass asked the convention, "What does [emancipation] amount to, if the Black man ... is to be subject to the slaveholder's shotgun?" The delegates were also unmoved by a woman, Sarah Spencer, who asked that women have the right to vote. Several days later, the Republican platform promised only "respectful consideration" of her request.

The most rousing speech at the 1876 convention was delivered by America's finest orator at the time, Colonel Robert Ingersoll of Illinois, who spoke in favor of Blaine. Calling him "a plumed knight" and a "leader of leaders," Ingersoll nominated Blaine "in the name of the great republic

. . . [and] her soldiers that died on the field of battle." Ingersoll's speech was so powerful that when he finished, Blaine's opponents adjourned the convention immediately to prevent the fired-up delegates from nominating Blaine on the first ballot.

By the next day, some of the enthusiasm for Blaine had cooled. For six ballots, Blaine won 40% of the votes, and Hayes and four other candidates divided the rest. Finally, on the seventh ballot, delegates from New York, Indiana, Kentucky, and Pennsylvania swung their votes to Hayes, giving him 384 delegates, five more than he needed to win the nomination.

Joseph Pulitzer, the publisher of the *New York World*, was not impressed. The party's logic, he said, is that "Hayes has never stolen. Good God, has it come to this?" The writer Henry Adams agreed, calling Hayes "a third-rate nonentity whose only recommendation is that he is obnoxious to no one." But President Ulysses Grant said, "Governor Hayes is a good selection and will make a good candidate."

During the autumn, Hayes and his running mate, Congressman William Wheeler of New York, supported gold-backed money, subsidies for the transcontinental railroads, and high tariffs to protect domestic factories. By contrast, Samuel Tilden stood for lower tariffs, stricter accounts of government spending, and "home rule" for the three Southern states that still had federal troops protecting unpopular Republican-led state governments. Tilden cautioned, however, that "no rebel debt will be assumed or paid" by the federal government and that "the questions settled by the [Civil] war are never to be reopened." "Let bygones be bygones," Tilden said, "turn from the dead past to a new and better future."

US troops were still in the South because the Ku Klux Klan and other vigilantes had intimidated Southern Blacks from voting. Hundreds of Blacks had been murdered and thousands more badly beaten. The Democratic Party never supported the attacks, but it clearly benefited from them because nearly all of the Blacks who stayed home from the polls would have voted Republican if they had the chance.

By 1876, with hardly any Blacks voting, most of the South was solidly Democratic again. Of the 16 states in the Deep South and Border South, 13 went for Tilden by a landslide. By contrast, most of the North was Republican. The Civil War was still recent, and speakers for Hayes "waved the bloody shirt." The famed orator Robert Ingersoll gave a particularly fiery speech:

> *Every man that shot Union soldiers was a Democrat . . . Every man*
> *that loved slavery better than liberty was a Democrat. The man that*
> *assassinated Abraham Lincoln was a Democrat. Every man that*
> *raised bloodhounds to pursue human beings was a Democrat. Soldiers,*
> *every scar you have on your heroic bodies was given you by a Democrat.*

Mark Twain also campaigned for Hayes.

Democrats focused on the need to end corruption. Holding bonfires and parades, Democrats across the country were more enthusiastic about Tilden than they had been about any candidate since Andrew Jackson. Compared to Hayes, Tilden seemed to have a sharper mind, a more detailed program, and more useful experience fighting graft.

On Election Day, four Northern swing states—New York, New Jersey, Connecticut, and Indiana—all went for Tilden as Irish immigrants helped Tilden outpoll Hayes nationally 50.9% to 47.9%, a solid lead of more than a quarter of a million votes. (Tilden's margin in Indiana, however, was only 1%.) With 185 electoral votes needed to win, the tally on election night was Tilden 184, Hayes 166, with Florida, Louisiana, and South Carolina, the last Southern states where Republicans still held office, too close to call. Tilden needed only one of these three states to win. Indeed, if Colorado had not been admitted as a state earlier in the year, Tilden would have won the election because his 184 electoral votes would have been a majority. Instead, Colorado cast three electoral votes for Hayes, and Tilden was one electoral vote short.

In New York, the Republican Party's national chairman, Zachariah Chandler, concluded that Tilden had beaten Hayes; Chandler then went to bed with a bottle of liquor to drown his sorrows. In Columbus, Ohio, Hayes also thought he had lost, telling his son, "I bow cheerfully to the result." Much less cheerful was Ohio Congressman James Garfield, the future president, who said that Tilden's apparent victory was a combination of "rebellion, Catholicism and whiskey." Across the nation, jubilant Democrats sent Tilden hundreds of congratulatory telegrams.

But Daniel Sickles, a former Union general who had lost a leg at Gettysburg, hobbled into the Republican Party's empty headquarters in Manhattan after an evening at the theater, read the latest election returns, and saw that Florida, Louisiana, and South Carolina were still undecided. Without any authorization, Sickles sent telegrams to each of the party chiefs there saying, "With your state sure for Hayes, he is elected. Hold your state." After this, the reporting of precincts from these three states slowed down considerably.

In Florida, the total from Dade County, which today includes Miami, was amusingly small: 9 votes for Hayes and 5 votes for Tilden. But in the rest of the Florida, the Republican-led vote-counting board brazenly threw out more than 1,500 votes for Tilden and declared Hayes the winner of the state by 922 votes. Within days, in a striking similarity to the year 2000, many of the nation's top lawyers rushed to Tallahassee, Florida's capital, to argue in courts about the state's vote count. One of these Republican lawyers was a former general, Lew Wallace, who would soon write *Ben-Hur: A Tale of the Christ*, America's best-selling novel after *Uncle Tom's Cabin* and before *Gone with the Wind*.

Louisiana made even Florida's clouded vote count look pristine. The state's Returning Board (whose members included a saloon keeper, an undertaker, and two plundering Northerners, all of whom would face criminal charges within a year) rejected more than 13,000 ballots for Tilden, including every single vote in two Democratic parishes, and declared that Hayes had won the state by 4,807 votes. And in South Carolina, a Republican-led election board also threw out more than 1,000 Tilden ballots, to give Hayes a statewide lead of 974 votes.

In each state, a Republican governor sent Congress a certificate declaring that Hayes had won all of the state's electoral votes. In Florida, however, a Democratic attorney general sent Congress a competing certificate that awarded Florida's votes to Tilden. In South Carolina the Democratic state legislature also sent Congress a certificate for Tilden, and in Louisiana a prominent Democrat who claimed to be the state's rightful governor sent a certificate for Tilden too.

Congress now had two sets of competing election certificates from Florida, Louisiana, and South Carolina. One set, preferred by the

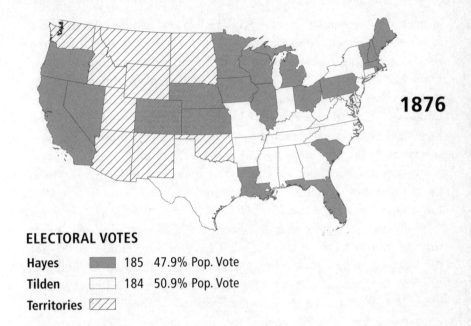

1876

ELECTORAL VOTES

Hayes — 185 47.9% Pop. Vote
Tilden — 184 50.9% Pop. Vote
Territories ⊘

Republicans who controlled the US Senate, awarded 19 electoral votes to Hayes. The other set, favored by the Democrats who controlled the House of Representatives, awarded the 19 votes to Tilden.

One electoral vote in Oregon was also in dispute because one of the Hayes electors there was a postmaster, and the US Constitution expressly forbids federal employees from serving as electors. The issue in Oregon was whether the Republican elector could simply resign as postmaster and remain an elector, or whether the state's Democratic governor could appoint someone from Tilden's slate of electors to serve instead, because Tilden had received the next highest number of votes in the state.

To avoid paralysis, the Republican Senate and the Democratic House of Representatives agreed in January 1877 to appoint a special electoral commission to decide which election certificates to honor and which to ignore. In 1877, unlike in 2000, no one questioned that it was primarily Congress rather than the Supreme Court that should decide the matter.

Fifteen men would serve on the Electoral Commission: five Republicans from Congress, five Democrats from Congress, and five associate justices of the Supreme Court—two Republicans, two Democrats, and a fifth justice who was an independent, David Davis of Illinois. Although President Lincoln had appointed Davis to the Supreme Court in 1862, Davis had strongly opposed the Radical Republicans during the Reconstruction Era, especially their attempt to impeach President Andrew Johnson in 1868. By 1877, Justice Davis was neither a Republican nor a Democrat, so everyone expected that he would cast the most impartial—and probably the deciding—vote on the commission.

By coincidence, however, only a few hours before Congress passed the bill that created the Electoral Commission, the Illinois state legislature chose Davis to be the state's junior US senator. In response, Davis, to avoid the appearance that a political deal had won him this Senate seat, refused to serve on the Electoral Commission. Unfortunately for the Democrats, the only Supreme Court justices left were Republicans, so when the next judge, Justice Joseph Bradley (appointed by President Grant in 1870), replaced Davis on the Electoral Commission, the Republicans enjoyed an 8-to-7 majority.

For weeks the Electoral Commission's 15 men argued about whether they had the authority to "go behind the returns" and investigate the clear bias of Florida's and South Carolina's vote-counting boards and the shameless conduct of Louisiana's Returning Board, which had thrown out more than 13,000 votes for Tilden. Uncharacteristically, the Republicans argued that vote-counting was a state matter, beyond the authority of the federal government, and said that to allow Congress to re-tabulate a state's votes would set a precedent far more dangerous than a mere failure to correct some instances of fraud.

Finally, by an 8-to-7 party-line vote, the Electoral Commission chose not to question any of the election certificates sent by the Republican governors of Florida, South Carolina, and Louisiana. (Ten years later, Congress confirmed this decision with an 1887 statute, still the law today, that requires Congress to accept a slate of electors that is certified by a state's governor unless both houses of Congress vote separately that the slate was elected fraudulently.)

Oregon presented a different problem because its governor, a Democrat, had certified that the state's electoral vote was Hayes 2, Tilden 1.

Unfazed, the Electoral Commission ruled, again by an 8-to-7 vote, that under Oregon law the proper authority to certify the electoral vote was not the governor but Oregon's Republican secretary of state, who had ruled that the state's electoral vote was Hayes 3, Tilden 0.

Outraged Democrats urged their senators to launch a filibuster to prevent the Electoral Commission from electing Hayes, but Tilden telegrammed congressional Democrats that he wanted the commission's count completed. Still, parliamentary delays by Democrats slowed down the Electoral Commission and kept it in session all through February, with President Grant's term set to end March 4.

At last, by another 8-to-7 vote, the Electoral Commission awarded all 20 of the disputed electoral votes to Hayes. The final total, 185 electoral votes for Rutherford B. Hayes and 184 for Samuel Tilden, was announced on March 2, 1877, at 4:10 in the morning, during an all-night session of Congress that ended just two days before the next president was due to be inaugurated.

The *New York Sun* said, "A man whom the people rejected at the polls has been declared President of the United States through processes of fraud. A cheat is to sit in the seat of George Washington." Cincinnati's *Enquirer* said, "Hayes is 'Commissioned' as President, and the monster fraud of the century is consummated." Other newspapers called the new president "His Fraudulency" or "Rutherfraud B. Hayes."

Some angry Democrats urged Tilden to hold his own inauguration and swear a separate oath of office. Others began to arm themselves, crying, "Tilden or blood!" But Tilden would have none of it. "I will never be a party to any course which will array my countrymen in civil war," he said, and most Democrats, although furious that the election had been stolen, admired his restraint.

After Hayes was inaugurated, Tilden joked that he had the honor of being elected president without the burden of the job's responsibilities. He spent the spring of 1877 reading several biographies of Oliver Cromwell, the Puritan general who overthrew King Charles I.

On June 12, Tilden gave a speech at the Manhattan Club in New York:

The men who were elected by the people President and Vice President of the United States were 'counted out,' and the men who were not elected were 'counted in' . . . If my voice could reach throughout our country and be heard in the remotest hamlet, I would say: "Be of good cheer. The republic will live . . . The sovereignty of the people shall be rescued from this peril and re-established."

The 1876 election was unquestionably the most corrupt presidential contest in American history, although the candidates themselves were honest men. We will never know for sure how a genuinely fair election that year would have turned out. A good guess is that in both Florida and South Carolina, enough Blacks would have voted Republican to tip the states' 11 electoral votes to Hayes. In Louisiana, however, where the state's Republican-controlled Returning Board nullified more than 13,000 votes for Tilden, Tilden's total may have been higher than Hayes's tally, even allowing for the additional number of Blacks who would have voted for Hayes had they felt that it was safe to do so.

A fair count of all the popular votes cast in 1876 would probably have led to an electoral vote of Tilden 195, Hayes 174, and possibly Tilden 203, Hayes 166. But a truly free election, where even Mississippi's Blacks, who were a majority of the state then, could have voted Republican, would probably have resulted in *four* Southern states going for Hayes, and an electoral vote of Hayes 193, Tilden 176.

The popular belief that Rutherford B. Hayes specifically promised Southern congressmen that he would remove federal troops from South Carolina and Louisiana in return for their acceptance of his election is an exaggeration, although it is true that 42 Southern Democratic congressmen agreed not to filibuster the election results, and Hayes did remove the last US soldiers from the South only a month and a half after his inauguration. But the Northern public had long been tired of keeping troops in the South, and President Grant, the outgoing incumbent, had already withdrawn many regiments. Even the great Black author and former slave, Frederick Douglass, conceded that the removal of federal

---

* Captain Franklin Ellis, *History of Columbia County, New York* (Philadelphia: Everts & Ensign, 1878), 8–9.

troops from the South was unfortunate but unavoidable. If Hayes had lost the election, Tilden would have removed the troops too.

The South's Democratic governors promised the Northern public that they would protect the civil rights of Black men and women, but not one governor kept his word. Without any Northern soldiers to protect them, Southern Blacks suffered 90 years of despotism. Blacks were not permitted to vote, own property, or get a decent education. As W. E. B. Du Bois wrote, "The slave went free; stood a brief moment in the sun; then moved back again toward slavery."

The US Supreme Court was no help. In 1883 it declared that the 1875 Civil Rights Act, which prohibited any discrimination against Blacks in public places, was unconstitutional despite the 14th Amendment's clear language that Congress can enforce equal rights for citizens with legislation. The Supreme Court said instead that while Congress could stop state governments from discriminating against Blacks, it could not prevent privately owned businesses from doing so. Blacks were barred from stores and had to ride in separate train cars for another 81 years, until Congress finally passed a new civil rights law in 1964.

1880

Four years later, the election was even closer. President Hayes, a Republican, had pledged to serve only one term, which was just as well because with the Democrats in control of both houses of Congress, there was not much he could accomplish anyway, although the White House did get its first telephone. Tilden, increasingly stiff and hoarse, lost his chance to run for president again when an investigation revealed that his nephew, without Tilden's knowledge, had tried to bribe some Southern vote-counting boards.

The Republican candidate for president in 1880 was a close friend of Hayes, James Garfield, an Ohio congressman who had served on the Electoral Commission in 1877 before becoming the Republican Minority Leader of the House of Representatives. As a teenager, Garfield had been a "tow boy," driving the mules that pulled the barges along the Ohio Canal. He then spent a decade at what is now Hiram College, first as a student, then as a professor of Greek and Latin, and finally, when he was only 26, as the president of the college.

Favoring high tariffs and civil service reform, Garfield ran for president against a Democrat, General Winfield Hancock, who had led troops in both the Mexican and Civil Wars. Garfield beat Hancock by less than ⅛ of 1% of the popular vote (4.54 million votes to 4.44 million), a margin of only 9,464 votes out of nearly 9 million cast. But the electoral vote was lopsided: Garfield 214, Hancock 155, because Garfield won the swing states of New York, Indiana, and Connecticut. Although the popular vote was razor-close, there was a clear winner as president within a day of the election, so the nation avoided the uncertainty that it had endured in 1876.

CHAPTER 4

The Loser Wins Again

Benjamin Harrison (1888)

WHEN PRESIDENT GROVER CLEVELAND RAN FOR REELECTION IN 1888, he won 90,000 more popular votes than his Republican opponent, Benjamin Harrison of Indiana, to no avail. It was Harrison who won the electoral vote, 233 to 168, and became America's 23rd president.

Born in 1833, Benjamin Harrison was named for his great-grandfather, who had cosigned the Declaration of Independence before becoming governor of Virginia. A still more distant Harrison ancestor was part of the Jamestown colony.

Benjamin's grandfather was William Henry Harrison, who became the nation's ninth president when Benjamin was seven. Harrison had fought Shawnee warriors in Indiana in 1811 and battled the British near Detroit during the War of 1812 before winning the 1840 presidential election a generation later. (If Harrison had won Illinois in 1840, which went for Martin Van Buren instead, Abraham Lincoln, a young supporter of Harrison, would have been one of the state's electors.)

Sadly, young Benjamin never got to see his grandfather in the White House because President Harrison died of pneumonia after only one month in office. The illness was made worse by doctors prescribing arsenic, among other toxins.

William Henry Harrison's third son, John, Benjamin's father, inherited a 600-acre farm in North Bend, Ohio, a few miles west of Cincinnati. With nine children to support, money was tight. Young Benjamin loved to hunt and fish to add food to the family's table, and might have remained an ordinary farm boy were it not for the fact that his grandfather's farmhouse contained hundreds of books. Benjamin liked to read about ancient and American history, and enjoyed adventure novels such as *Ivanhoe*. In a high school essay, Harrison wrote that you can judge a civilization by how its men treat their women. Women "are appreciated in proportion as society is advanced."

The hardworking Harrison graduated third in his class at Miami University of Ohio, where he studied history and excelled in debating. Then he spent two years reading law in Cincinnati. At 20, he married Caroline Scott, also 20, the daughter of the president of a nearby women's college, the Oxford Female Institute.

In 1854 Harrison inherited $800 from an aunt and used the money to move to Indianapolis, which was then a small but growing town of 16,000 people. As a young lawyer, Harrison prepared his cases in great detail, but late one afternoon, when the courthouse light was unusually dim, he discovered that he was a more lively speaker when he did not use any notes.

At first, Harrison had few clients. He made some money as a judge's "crier," calling a court into session, then won a job with a prominent law firm before he was elected city attorney in 1857. Three years later, during the 1860 campaign, Harrison made 80 speeches for Abraham Lincoln. If he was introduced as the grandson of President William Henry Harrison, however, he said, "I am the grandson of nobody. I believe every man should stand on his own merits."

When the Civil War began, Harrison did not volunteer at first because he was supporting three children and a nephew, and like everyone else he thought the war would be over soon. But by the summer of 1862, when he was recruiting soldiers, Harrison realized that he could not ask others to do something that he was not also going to do himself. Harrison enlisted as a second lieutenant but continued to recruit troops, and soon became the colonel of a new regiment that he had personally formed, drilled, and disciplined: the 70th Indiana Infantry.

Harrison described himself as a "plain Hoosier colonel" and "a good soldier of Jesus Christ." He led prayers at campsites, but also learned to drink a little when it was time for a toast. During 1862 and 1863 Harrison and his men merely guarded fortifications in Kentucky and Tennessee, but this gave him the time he needed to read military books and train his men. By 1864 the 70th Infantry was helping General Sherman advance to Atlanta. In fact, during that bloody summer Harrison led his troops into more battles in one month than his presidential grandfather, William Henry, the hero of the Battle of Tippecanoe, had fought in his entire life. Because the pale, blond-haired Harrison was only five-feet-six, his men called him "Little Ben," but by the time the war ended, "Little Ben" was a brigadier general.

Returning home to Indianapolis, Harrison became one of the city's best lawyers, but also taught Sunday school at a Presbyterian church. In 1876, when a scandal forced the Republican nominee for governor to withdraw from the race, Harrison agreed to run even though the Democratic candidate had a big lead. Harrison's opponent described himself as a simple farm boy running against a big-city lawyer, "Blue Jeans" versus "Kid Gloves." Harrison, who did wear gloves as well as a top hat (to add to his height), surprised everyone by coming within 1.1% of victory, and soon he was the leader of Indiana's Republican Party.

In 1880 Harrison campaigned hard for James Garfield, and the next year Indiana's state legislature made Harrison a US senator. In Washington, Harrison favored civil service reform and opposed a bill that excluded Chinese immigrants. He also tried to improve schools for southern Blacks, but every time an education bill passed in the Republican Senate, it was defeated in the Democratic House.

In 1881, during Harrison's first year in the Senate, President Garfield was shot by a mentally ill job-seeker only four months after his inauguration, and died in September. Garfield's successor, Chester Alan Arthur, served only one term as president and did not run for reelection in 1884. The significant civil service reform that President Arthur pushed and signed into law was long overdue, but it alienated the Republican Party's bosses, who had preferred to make political appointments, so there was little chance of Arthur's winning the Republican presidential nomination at a convention.

Some people mocked Arthur as the "Dude President" because he owned 25 different overcoats. He was also unpopular with reporters because he rarely gave interviews or paused for photographs. "I may be President of the United States," he once said, "but my private life is nobody's damn business."

1884

As President Arthur's prospects for staying in office dimmed, many Republicans talked of nominating William Tecumseh Sherman, the Union commander who had captured Atlanta and marched across Georgia, until finally the general put an end to the idea with his immortal refusal: "If nominated, I will not accept. If elected, I will not serve." In the end, the candidates in 1884 were New York's Democratic governor, Grover Cleveland, and Maine's Republican senator, James G. Blaine.

The election of 1884 was almost as close as the election of 1880, but had much more memorable slogans. The best rhyme started when two newspapers revealed that Governor Cleveland was paying child support to an attractive mother of an illegitimate boy in Buffalo. The boy was probably the son of Cleveland's best friend and law partner, Oscar Folsom, who had died when he was thrown from a carriage; Cleveland wanted to spare the widow and her 11-year-old daughter, who knew nothing about Folsom's affair, from embarrassment. But Republicans across the country were skeptical of this explanation, and pushed baby carriages in town squares, chanting, "Ma! Ma! Where's my pa?" Democrats, not to be outdone, pointed to questionable financial dealings by Senator Blaine and jeered back, "Blaine, Blaine, James G. Blaine, the continental liar from the state of Maine!"

On Election Day, Cleveland won 48.9% of the vote, and Blaine won 48.3%. The swing states, including New York, went Democratic this time, because with the Civil War 20 years past, more people were willing to accept a Democrat as president again. A shift of only 575 votes, however, would have kept New York in the Republican column and made Blaine president. With New York going Democratic, Cleveland won 54% of the electoral votes, so once again the nation had a clear winner even before all the popular votes were counted.

Democrats, answering the Republican chant, "Ma! Ma! Where's my pa?" triumphantly replied, "Gone to the White House, ha, ha, ha!"

Grover Cleveland, a descendant of the founders of Cleveland, Ohio, was a big man, nearly six feet tall and 270 pounds. His nephews and nieces affectionately called him "Uncle Jumbo." A bachelor until he was president, Cleveland worked long hours, then washed down a big dinner with some beer in the evening. Despite his size, he had a modern look. At a time when most men wore beards, Cleveland had only a mustache.

Born in 1837, Cleveland was the fifth of nine children of a low-salaried but Yale-educated Presbyterian minister. He grew up in Fayetteville, New York, east of Syracuse, and worked in a grocery store for a dollar a week while studying Latin and mathematics in the evening by the light of an oil lamp. When he was 16, his father died, which ended any chance of his having enough money to go to college.

At 18, on his way to Ohio, Cleveland stopped to visit relatives in Buffalo, where an uncle found him a job as a clerk at former president Millard Fillmore's law firm. Four years later Cleveland was admitted to the New York Bar. His salary increased, but Cleveland continued to send most of it to his mother, who was still raising children.

During the Civil War, Cleveland worked as a prosecutor. Because his entire family was dependent on him, he avoided the draft by paying $150 to a Polish immigrant to take his place in the army, and another $150 to the government. This was a common practice during the war, and the substitute survived.

Cleveland started his own law firm in 1869 and was elected sheriff of Erie County in 1870. Twice, while he was sheriff, he pulled the lever at the gallows to hang a convicted murderer, explaining that he could not ask a deputy to do a job just because he didn't want to do it himself. For a while some Republican opponents called him the Buffalo Hangman.

Buffalo was a booming city in the 19th century, with busy docks and factories manned by thousands of German and Irish workmen. In the evening, they liked to drink beer in saloons. As a rising young politician, Cleveland sometimes climbed on top of a beer barrel to talk about local politics with the laborers, most of whom were happy to listen to him because they were illiterate and could not read a newspaper. Often Cleveland made them laugh by mimicking other politicians.

In 1881, when Cleveland ran for mayor, he gave dozens of speeches in the back rooms of waterfront taverns. After he won, he surprised everyone by awarding city contracts not to his political allies, but to the lowest bidder. He said "no" to so many bloated, pork-filled contracts that he quickly became known as the "Veto Mayor." Only one year later, voters who were disgusted with corrupt bosses and hungry for honest politicians elected Cleveland governor of New York by a landslide over a Republican candidate who was too closely associated with Jay Gould, the notorious railroad tycoon.

As governor, Cleveland read every law he signed, and even worked on Sundays for a few hours before playing some poker. He was always in the mainstream of public opinion in the state. He signed a law that banned child labor in cigar factories, but opposed a bill that would have limited the workdays of trolley car conductors to 12 hours. His free-market argument was that the conductors had the right to work as many hours as they pleased. Cleveland continued to veto public works bills that were too expensive, and preserved land in the Adirondacks and at Niagara Falls. He also signed a law making New York City's employees answerable to the mayor rather than to the more corrupt local aldermen.

In 1884 Democrats north and south jumped at the chance to have a presidential candidate from New York, with its 36 electoral votes, who was free from any tie to New York City's corrupt Tammany Hall machine. Cleveland was neither a war hero nor popular with party bosses, but his reputation for integrity was so strong that at the party's convention in Chicago, he won 48% of the delegates on the first ballot and 83% of them on the second.

After Cleveland won the presidential nomination, and Indiana's racist governor Thomas Hendricks received the vice presidential nod, the band played "For He's a Jolly Good Fellow" and then "Praise God, from Whom All Blessings Flow." When Cleveland received the news of his nomination by telegraph at the Governor's Mansion in Albany, he merely said, "By Jove, that is something, isn't it?"

Both parties favored high tariffs and restrictions on Chinese immigration, but the Democrats also supported the right of workers to form unions. Cleveland, following custom, did not campaign, but spent most of the autumn in Albany.

In New York City, six days before the presidential election, a Presbyterian minister, Samuel Burchard, introduced the Republican candidate, James G. Blaine, to a gathering of clergymen at the Fifth Avenue Hotel and blasted the Democrats as the party of "Rum, Romanism and Rebellion." Blaine, who was not paying attention, did not denounce the remark until the next day, when it was too late. Democrats made sure the slur was printed in every newspaper in America, and it particularly offended New York's Irish Catholics, who responded by voting in record numbers.

Reverend Burchard's catchy phrase cost the Republicans the election. Cleveland won New York by only 1,149 votes out of more than a million cast and, nationally, squeaked past Blaine, with 4.87 million votes to Blaine's 4.85 million. In addition to winning a solid South, Cleveland took New York, New Jersey, Connecticut, and Indiana, and won the electoral vote, 219 to 182. Cleveland was the first Democrat to be elected president in 28 years, since before the Civil War.

In the White House, Cleveland worked most evenings, and for dinner often preferred what his servants were eating to the "French stuff" that his chefs liked to cook. He stayed in the mainstream of national public opinion too. He signed the Interstate Commerce Act to regulate the railroads, but vetoed an emergency bill that would have bought seeds for drought-stricken farmers in Texas. "Though the people support the government," he said, "the government should not support the people."

Cleveland also vetoed hundreds of pork-barrel construction projects, and ended government pensions for veterans' widows if the widows remarried. Regrettably, as the South's discriminatory Jim Crow laws grew ever harsher, Cleveland offered southern Blacks no help at all.

⁓

In 1886 Benjamin Harrison campaigned hard for Republican state legislators in Indiana, and bought a mimeograph machine to "multiply my letters." In November the Republican candidates for Indiana's legislature won 10,000 more votes than the Democrats did. Because of gerrymandering, however, Indiana's Democrats won several more seats than the Republicans, and the new legislature chose a Democrat to replace Harrison as US senator.

Still, politicians everywhere knew that it was the Republicans who had won the most votes in Indiana—the second-biggest swing state after New York—so once James G. Blaine announced that he would not run for president in 1888, Harrison immediately became one of the leading candidates for the Republican presidential nomination at the party's convention in Chicago.

1888

When the front-runner at the Republican Convention, Ohio's Senator John Sherman, the brother of the famous general, failed to win more than a third of the vote after six ballots, Blaine swung his support to Harrison, who had campaigned for Blaine when he ran for president in 1884. On the seventh ballot Harrison pulled ahead of Sherman, and on the eighth ballot he won the presidential nomination by an overwhelming majority. The delegates also nominated New York's Levi Morton, a banker, former congressman, and former ambassador to France, for vice president. (After winning the presidency, Harrison rewarded Blaine for his support by appointing him secretary of state. Harrison probably knew that he would have an easier time leading the Republican Party with Blaine inside his cabinet rather than outside it.)

Although tradition kept presidential candidates from actively campaigning in the 19th century, Harrison began a low-key "front-porch" campaign, giving daily speeches to friendly crowds at a park near his home. In the evening, he read a stenographer's transcript of his talk carefully, and sometimes made small changes before releasing the speech to newspapers.

The biggest issue in 1888 was whether the government's many tariffs on imports should be lowered. Harrison favored high tariffs that made European goods more expensive, because this allowed American companies to compete with their European rivals more easily. Without high tariffs, Republicans said, European products would be much cheaper than

US goods, because European workers received lower wages than Americans did. In fact, despite the difference in wages, American products were usually cheaper than European goods because of more modern production techniques.

Unlike Harrison, President Cleveland wanted to lower the tariffs on foreign goods to make things cheaper for American consumers, especially because the federal government was already collecting about $100 million more each year than it spent. In December 1887, Cleveland devoted his entire State of the Union message to a request that Congress reduce the nation's import duties. The bill passed the House of Representatives, but died in committee in the Senate.

William Whitney, Cleveland's secretary of the navy, warned the president that calling for reduced tariffs would hurt his chances of winning New York in the next election, because northern businessmen liked the tariffs, and even factory workers believed that without high tariffs their wages would fall.

Whitney was right. Cleveland lost New York in 1888 even though it was his home state, and this cost him the election (just as Al Gore's loss of his home state of Tennessee cost him the election in 2000). Although Harrison won New York by only 1% of the popular vote, he received all 36 of its electoral votes. Harrison also took Indiana, his home state, by only ⁹⁄₁₀ of 1% of the vote, a state that Cleveland had narrowly won in 1884.

The Deep South and Border South were solid for Cleveland, but the only northern states that Cleveland won in 1888 were New Jersey and Connecticut (where the president's margin was just 336 votes), and they were not enough.

Although Cleveland surpassed Harrison in the nation's popular vote, 48.6% to 47.8% (a Prohibition candidate also won 2.2% of the ballots), too many of Cleveland's votes were wasted in landslides in the South. Harrison's narrower but more numerous victories in the North and West enabled him to win the electoral vote by a decisive margin, 233 to 168, so he became the nation's 23rd president. (If New York, Grover Cleveland's home state, had remained Democratic, the electoral vote would have been Cleveland 204, Harrison 197.)

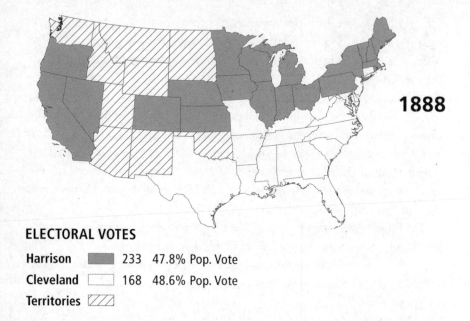

1888

ELECTORAL VOTES

Harrison	�	233	47.8% Pop. Vote
Cleveland	☐	168	48.6% Pop. Vote
Territories	▨		

The 1888 election was the last time that a second-place candidate won the electoral vote and the presidency until 2000, when George W. Bush also became president with fewer popular votes than his opponent.*

As was true in 1876, the Democrats could hardly complain about the injustice of losing the electoral vote in 1888 because southern Democrats had prevented many thousands of mostly Republican Blacks from voting, and these votes almost certainly would have given Harrison a popular-vote majority.

---

* The presidential election of 1916 almost had an outcome similar to that of 1888. President Woodrow Wilson, running for reelection, won enormous landslides in the South, taking 97% of the vote in South Carolina, 93% in Mississippi, and 86% in Louisiana. By contrast, Wilson's Republican opponent, Charles Evans Hughes, won Indiana and West Virginia by less than 1% of the vote, and Minnesota by only 1/10 of 1%. The final national tally showed Wilson with 49.2% of the popular vote and 277 electoral votes, and Hughes with 46.1% of the popular vote and 254 electoral votes. But in California, a switch of just 1/8 of 1% of the vote from Wilson to Hughes (1,287 votes out of a million cast) would have flipped California's 13 electoral votes from Wilson to Hughes, and the nation's totals would have been Hughes, with 46.1% of the popular vote and 267 electoral votes defeating Wilson, with 49.2% of the popular vote and 264 electoral votes. Charles Evans Hughes, who like Benjamin Harrison was a second-place candidate favored by the northern industrial states, would then have become the nation's 29th president only one month before America's entry into World War I.

Harrison did manage to win 49.5% of the vote in Virginia and more than 47% of the vote in Maryland and North Carolina. If more Blacks had been able to vote in Virginia alone, Harrison would have won Virginia's 12 electoral votes—and the presidency—even without the 36 electoral votes that he took so narrowly in New York. With Virginia's 12 votes, Harrison would have had a total of 209 electoral votes (201 were needed to win), making New York unnecessary. So if the 1888 election had been fairer, Benjamin Harrison would still have defeated Grover Cleveland.

One month after his defeat, President Cleveland, in his last annual message to Congress, warned of the widening gulf between the "rich and powerful" and the "toiling poor." "Communism is a hateful thing and a menace to peace and organized government," the president said, "but the communism of combined wealth and capital . . . which insidiously undermines the justice and integrity of free institutions, is not less dangerous than the communism of oppressed poverty and toil."

On the morning of March 4, 1889, the last day of Cleveland's presidency, Cleveland's wife of three years, Frances Folsom Cleveland, spoke to the White House staff. The poised and educated daughter of Cleveland's deceased best friend, Oscar Folsom (who had probably fathered the illegitimate boy in Buffalo), had at 21 become the youngest First Lady in American history. In 1886 John Philip Sousa had led the US Marine Band at the White House wedding, and Queen Victoria and Kaiser Wilhelm I had telegraphed their congratulations. President Cleveland had also agreed that the word "obey" would not be a part of his bride's vows. Now, after nearly three years as First Lady, Frances told her servants with a smile, "Take good care of all the furniture and ornaments in the house, for I want to find everything just as it is now when we come back again. We are coming back just four years from today."

And they did.

At noon on the same day, President Harrison delivered his inaugural speech during a torrential rainstorm. Gallantly, Cleveland, a private citizen again, held an umbrella over the head of the nation's new Chief Executive.

One change at the White House during Harrison's presidency was the installation of electric lights, although most of the Harrisons were afraid to touch the switches for fear of being electrocuted. When the Clevelands returned to the White House in 1893, however, they were familiar with electricity, having lived in Manhattan. During Cleveland's four years in New York, he practiced law, enjoyed the theater, and fathered the first of his five children with Frances: Ruth, for whom the Baby Ruth candy bar would later be named. Unfortunately, Ruth died of diphtheria at the age of 12.

As president, Benjamin Harrison signed the Meat Inspection Act and the Sherman Antitrust Act in 1890 and the Forest Reserve Act in 1891, which set aside 13 million acres (an area almost the size of West Virginia) as national forest. But bowing to pressure from California's Republicans, Harrison reversed his stand on Chinese immigration and signed a law that banned any more immigrants from China for 10 years. Harrison also nearly doubled the number of Civil War veterans eligible for pensions, and soon pensions for veterans and their families accounted for 40% of the federal budget. When Democrats complained about a "Billion-Dollar Congress," Thomas Reed, the Republican Speaker of the House, replied, "This is a billion-dollar country!"

Harrison said that the lynchings of Blacks by white mobs "shame our Christian civilization." He also tried to win voting rights for Blacks. "It will not do," Harrison said, to say that voting "is a local question to be settled by the states." Harrison fought for a bill to hire inspectors to watch the voting in congressional elections, with the power to challenge an election if there were irregularities. The House passed the bill in 1890 by a strict party-line vote, 155 to 149. In the Senate, however, Republicans from the West saw a chance to win new allies in their quest for a silver-backed currency, and joined southern Democrats to defeat the bill on a procedural vote, 35 to 34. Colorado's Senator Edward Wolcott said, "There are many things more important and vital to the welfare of our nation than that the colored citizens of the South shall vote." Voting rights for southern Blacks had to wait another 75 years.

1892

By 1892 many workmen were becoming disenchanted with the Republican Party. They began to see labor rights as more important than tariffs, pensions, or race relations. A gun battle erupted in Homestead, Pennsylvania, that year when steelworkers, striking against wage cuts, fought detectives who were sent to put down the strike. When the shooting stopped, 12 people were dead and 60 wounded. Pennsylvania's governor sent troops to Homestead to restore order, and to end both the strike and the union that called it. But afterward, it was hard to argue that America's record-high tariffs on European steel and other foreign imports, which President Harrison and other Republicans favored, were helping ordinary laborers in the mills.

At the 1892 Republican Convention in Minneapolis, Harrison was renominated on the first ballot, and Whitelaw Reid, a former ambassador to France who owned the *New York Tribune*, was nominated for vice president. At the Democratic Party convention in Chicago, former president Grover Cleveland was nominated on the first ballot, and Adlai Stevenson of Illinois, the grandfather of the party's nominee in 1952 and 1956, won the vice presidential nomination.

On Election Day many working-class voters defected from the Republican Party and swung New York, Indiana, Illinois, and Wisconsin to the Democrats, giving Cleveland not just a 46% to 43% lead over President Harrison in the popular vote, but a massive majority of the electoral votes too, with 277 votes for Cleveland, 145 for Harrison, and 22 for Iowa's James Weaver, the Populist Party candidate. Grover Cleveland not only won the presidency a second time, he won the popular vote a *third* time, the only president besides Franklin Roosevelt to do this. The Democrats also took both houses of Congress for the first time since 1858, before the Civil War.

James Weaver, the Populist Party's leader, was a former Civil War general and congressman who fought for farmers and favored a silver-backed currency and a graduated income tax. He won five western states and received 8.5% of the popular vote, mostly from previously Republican farmers who were angry that banks were collecting high interest rates on loans and railroads were charging high prices to haul crops.

President Harrison did not campaign at all in 1892. His wife, Caroline, suffered from tuberculosis and died just two weeks before the election. When his term ended in March 1893, Harrison returned to Indianapolis to write a book on American government, *This Country of Ours*. Three years later, he married his deceased wife's niece.

The Democratic Party's triumph in 1892 was short-lived because in 1893 a financial panic led to a severe depression. President Cleveland persuaded Congress to repeal a disastrous 1890 law that had allowed people to exchange silver for gold and hoard the gold, but crop prices continued to fall, and one-fifth of the nation's factory workers lost their jobs.

The Republicans took back both houses of Congress in 1894, and the preference of voters in the East and Midwest for gold-backed rather than silver-backed currency led to Republican landslides in the next four presidential elections. Even President Cleveland, the nation's most prominent Democrat, said that silver-backed currency would be "dangerous and reckless." The outgoing president was appalled when William Jennings Bryan gave his famous speech for silver at the 1896 Democratic Convention: "We will answer their demand for a gold standard by saying to them: 'You shall not press down upon this brow of labor this crown of thorns— you shall not crucify mankind upon a cross of gold!'" Cleveland refused to endorse Bryan for president even though Bryan was the Democratic Party's nominee in 1896, 1900, and 1908.*

⸺

The 20-year period when the nation was evenly divided by its two major parties finally came to an end. Presidential elections would not be so close again until 1960, 1968, and 1976, when the two parties were once again briefly equal in strength as the era of Democratic dominance that began with Franklin Roosevelt was being replaced by an era of Republican supremacy under Ronald Reagan.

---

* In an article for the *Ladies' Home Journal* in October 1905, Cleveland also opposed women's suffrage. "Sensible and responsible women do not want to vote," Cleveland wrote. "The relative positions to be assumed by man and woman in working out civilization were assigned long ago by a higher intelligence than ours."

In our own time, the elections of 2000 and 2004 were razor-close, and in 2012 the popular vote was also competitive. It is too soon to tell whether we have entered another era when the parties are evenly divided, but if we have, the chance of another runner-up candidate winning the electoral vote and the presidency with fewer votes than his or her opponent in the next 30 years is better than even.

CHAPTER 5

The House Decides

Jefferson vs. Burr (1800)

THE 1800 PRESIDENTIAL ELECTION WAS THROWN TO THE HOUSE OF Representatives, with each state, however large or small, having one vote. Two men had run for president: John Adams, running for reelection, and Thomas Jefferson. Adams lost, but the race shifted to the House of Representatives because the election ended as a tie between Thomas Jefferson and his vice presidential running mate, Aaron Burr. At the time, each presidential elector cast two votes for president, instead of one vote for president and one vote for vice president as electors do today. Yet not one of the 73 electors who voted for Jefferson took the precaution of not casting his second vote for Burr, so Burr received 73 electoral votes for president too, just as Jefferson did.

Because of this tie, the election moved to the House of Representatives. Before the Constitution's 12th Amendment was ratified in 1804, a presidential election could shift to the House in one of two ways. First, if no one received a majority of the electoral votes, then the House would choose a president from among the top five electoral-vote winners. But second, if two men won electoral-vote majorities of precisely the same size, as happened with Jefferson and Burr, then the House had to choose one of the two men as president.

In the House of Representatives, Jefferson's enemies were called Federalists because they wanted a strong federal government, and they gleefully embraced the new opportunity to try to deny Jefferson the presidency. Their efforts nearly led to civil war, which is why Congress, before the next presidential election was held in 1804, passed the 12th Amendment to create separate electoral contests for president and vice president, and also why the states ratified the amendment so quickly. More than 210 years have passed since the 12th Amendment was enacted, but no attempt to reform our electoral system by amending the Constitution has ever been successful again, despite hundreds of tries.

———

When the Founding Fathers wrote the Constitution in 1787, giving each elector two votes for president seemed like a good idea. The elector would cast one vote for a favorite son from his own state, and the other vote for someone worthy from another state. Casting two votes for president would encourage electors to vote in the interest of the entire nation, not just their own region. The Framers hoped that the most qualified man would win the most votes and become president, and the second-most qualified man would win the second-most votes and become vice president. (They did not foresee the rise of political parties, although by the time George Washington retired in 1797, parties had formed quickly.)

Unfortunately, a problem arose when candidates for president and vice president began to run together as a ticket. The electors continued to cast two votes for president, but there was no way at the time to differentiate between a vote for the presidential candidate and a vote for his running mate.

Still, the Constitution worked reasonably well in 1796, when John Adams was elected president with 71 electoral votes and Thomas Jefferson was chosen vice president with 68 electoral votes, although for the next four years it was awkward to have the vice president lead the opposition to the president. (Picture Mitt Romney as Obama's vice president.)

———

Adams's greatest achievement as president was avoiding what almost certainly would have been a disastrous war with France. During the Napoleonic War between France and Britain, French sea captains captured many American merchant ships that were sailing to Britain and confiscated their cargo. Many Americans were outraged and wanted to go to war, but in the 1790s the United States had no standing army and no navy at all. President Adams responded to the French naval seizures by forming an army of 10,000 men and building a navy of 50 ships, but he also sent John Marshall and Charles Cotesworth Pinckney to Paris to try to negotiate a treaty of neutrality with France.

They succeeded, but too late to help Adams win reelection. On October 3, 1800, US and French diplomats signed a treaty that ended the French seizures of American ships, although the French did not have to reimburse any American merchants for the cargo that they had already confiscated. Unfortunately for Adams, the details of this peace agreement did not reach America until December, well after everyone had voted.

Adams's greatest mistake as president was to sign the Sedition Act on July 14, 1798. It was a clear violation of the First Amendment because the act made it illegal, on pain of fines and imprisonment, to "write, print, utter or publish" anything "false, scandalous and malicious" against the president or Congress, or bring "them into contempt or disrepute." The House of Representatives had only narrowly passed the bill, 44 to 41, with the support of just two southerners.

Abigail Adams, tired of reading newspaper articles that falsely described her husband as old, whining, and toothless, had strongly encouraged Adams to sign the Sedition Act. Samuel Dana, a Federalist congressman from Connecticut, also favored the act, asking, "How could the rights of the people require a liberty to utter falsehoods?"

The federal government arrested 25 people for sedition, including Benjamin Franklin Bache, a Philadelphia newspaperman and grandson of Benjamin Franklin who died of a fever before his trial, and Matthew Lyon, a Vermont congressman who served four months in prison before voters reelected him by a landslide. The government also arrested Luther Baldwin of Newark, New Jersey, because when President and Mrs. Adams rode a carriage out of town as cannon boomed in their honor, he had drunkenly shouted, "There goes the president and they are firing at his ass!" He was fined $200.

Thomas Jefferson hated the Sedition Act. In 1787 he wrote, "Were it left for me to decide whether we should have a government without newspapers or newspapers without a government, I should not hesitate a moment to prefer the latter." Now, 11 years later, Jefferson proposed a resolution for the Kentucky legislature that claimed that "every state has a natural right . . . to nullify of their own authority all assumptions of powers not expressly listed in the Constitution." The Kentucky declaration never came to a vote, however, and when James Madison drafted a similar resolution in Virginia, he left out the frightening word "nullify."

The soft-spoken Jefferson, who was six-feet-two-inches tall in an age when most men were short, appeared even more striking because he had red hair and freckles. He played the violin; read French, Greek, and Latin; and invented a swivel chair. Jefferson had his slaves grow 70 different kinds of vegetables in a garden 1,000 feet long. They also worked as carpenters; wove cloth; tended orchards; and ran a sawmill, a smokehouse, and a nail factory.

For many years, Jefferson and Adams had worked well together. In 1776, although Jefferson was the chief author of the Declaration of Independence, Adams and three other men, Benjamin Franklin, Roger Sherman, and Robert Livingston, helped edit it. Years later, Adams claimed that he was the one who had insisted that Jefferson be the Declaration's principal author: "Reason 1st. You are a Virginian, and a Virginian ought to appear as the head of this business. Reason 2nd. I am obnoxious, suspected and unpopular. You are very much otherwise. Reason 3rd. You can write ten times better than I can."

Later, Jefferson and Adams were diplomats together in Paris, and when Washington was president, Adams was vice president while Jefferson was secretary of state. In 1796, however, both men competed to be Washington's successor. Adams won the presidential election by only three electoral votes.

In 1800 Jefferson challenged Adams again. He promised not only to repeal the Sedition Act, but also to reduce taxes and spending by allowing state militias to replace the new national army. It was an ugly campaign. Newspapers that supported Jefferson described Adams as an aristocrat who looked down on people, which was ironic because Adams was the son of an ordinary farmer while Jefferson had inherited 2,500 acres and hundreds of slaves. Many newspapers also portrayed Adams as a madman with a volcanic temper.

Federalist newspapers and preachers called Jefferson an atheist. In *Notes on the State of Virginia*, Jefferson had once written, "It does me no injury for my neighbor to say there are twenty gods, or no god. It neither picks my pocket nor breaks my leg." But Jefferson's tolerant outlook scandalized many clergymen because it reduced their rocklike Christian faith to a mere matter of opinion. Twenty years later, after he retired, Jefferson also cut and pasted his own version of the Gospels, leaving out the miracles. He called it *The Life and Morals of Jesus of Nazareth* and often read it before he went to bed.

"No one knows," the *Connecticut Courant* warned, "whether Mr. Jefferson believes in one God, or in many; or in none at all." The *Courant* predicted that if the Virginian "atheist" won the presidency, "murder, robbery, rape, adultery, and incest will all be openly taught and practiced." Some preachers even warned their congregations to hide their Bibles if Jefferson became president.

This was also ironic, because Adams was a freethinker too. Writing in his diary at the age of 20, Adams had speculated that the existence of intelligent life on other planets would make Christian doctrine awkward. "EITHER God Almighty must assume the respective shapes of all these different Species, and suffer the penalties of their Crimes in their stead; OR ELSE all these Beings must be consigned to everlasting Perdition?"* Adams was annoyed by the constant attempts by clerics to drag Jefferson's religion into the campaign. "What does that have to do with the public?" he asked.

Although newspapers were harsh, Adams and Jefferson themselves kept silent. Even the slightest campaigning by a presidential candidate then would have seemed vulgar. Until the era of William Jennings Bryan and Theodore Roosevelt, a national candidate was supposed to stay above the fray. During the autumn of 1800, while Jefferson's supporters worked long and hard for his election, Jefferson himself remained at Monticello, supervising a wheat harvest and writing a manual on parliamentary procedure.

To no one's surprise, New Englanders preferred Adams while southerners favored Jefferson. The battleground was in the Middle Atlantic

---

* Richard Holmes, *The Age of Wonder* (New York: Vintage Books, 2008), 167.

states. Jefferson had support there among farmers, workmen, and immigrants, but in 1800 people could only vote for their presidential electors in five states. In the other 11, including the pivotal states of New York and Pennsylvania, it was the state legislators, not the voters, who chose the electors.

In Pennsylvania, pro-Adams Federalists held a majority in the state's senate while Jefferson's followers, the Democratic-Republicans, controlled the state's house of representatives. (The Democratic-Republicans were called "Republicans" for short, which is confusing today because Jefferson's "Republican" party eventually became the modern Democratic Party. The modern Republican Party did not form until 1854.)

With Pennsylvania's two houses split, legislators were deadlocked. In a compromise, they finally agreed to cast eight electoral votes for Jefferson and seven for Adams. The one-vote margin made Pennsylvania's role in the 1800 election irrelevant.

Everything hinged on New York and South Carolina. People knew that New York's 12 electors would probably decide the presidential election, so the local elections for state senators and assemblymen suddenly had national significance. Because upstate New York's districts were evenly divided between the Federalists and the Republicans, it was New York City's legislative elections that would determine the outcome.

Alexander Hamilton crisscrossed the city to make speeches for Federalist candidates, but it was Aaron Burr's campaigning that was truly extraordinary. The son of a minister who headed a college that eventually became Princeton University, Burr had served bravely during the Revolutionary War, although Washington prophetically wrote that Burr had "talents at intrigue." After the war, Burr was elected to the New York State Assembly, and later to the US Senate.

In April 1800, Burr launched the world's first modern political campaign. He had volunteers knock on doors throughout Manhattan and made sure that campaign workers had plenty to eat and mattresses to sleep on at Burr's luxurious Wall Street home. He also sent German-speakers to campaign for Jefferson in the city's new and fast-growing German neighborhoods, while in the city's older districts, Burr made speeches himself praising Jefferson and the Republican candidates.

In a huge embarrassment for the Federalists, Jedidiah Peck, a New York assemblyman who had been arrested, handcuffed, and indicted under the Sedition Act because he had condemned the law as an evil attempt to "convert Freemen into Slaves," was scheduled to be tried in New York City in April. Most voters saw Peck as a martyr, suffering for the cause of free speech. Federalist prosecutors, finally realizing that their trial was a tremendous blunder, dropped the charges.

On Election Day, April 30, Burr arranged for hundreds of carriages, wagons, and drivers to take elderly voters to the polls, and also sent poll watchers to monitor the collection and counting of the ballots. His work paid off. By narrow margins, the Republican candidates swept New York City. And now that the Republicans had a solid majority in the state legislature, New York's 12 electoral votes, which had been cast for Adams in 1796, would go to Jefferson instead in 1800. "The Goddess of Liberty has put to flight the demon of Aristocracy," gloated one upstate New York newspaper.

"We have beat you by superior management," Burr told a downcast Federalist, and Burr's effort was soon rewarded. Jefferson needed a northerner as his vice presidential running mate, and on May 11 a caucus of Republican congressmen formally nominated Jefferson and Burr to run together in the coming presidential election. President Adams, a New Englander, took a running mate from South Carolina: Charles Cotesworth Pinckney, a Revolutionary War general who later attended the Constitutional Convention and served as the US Minister to France.

States did not vote on the same day until 1845, and in 1800 the last state to choose its presidential electors was South Carolina, where the legislature waited until December 2 to make its selection. By then, Adams had won 65 electoral votes (and Pinckney 64) from New England, New Jersey, and half of Pennsylvania and Maryland, while Jefferson and Burr had each won 65 electoral votes from New York, five southern states, and the other halves of Pennsylvania and Maryland. South Carolina's eight electors would therefore decide the election, but although most of the South was solidly for Jefferson, the city of Charleston remained Federalist.

Alexander Hamilton despised both President Adams for making peace with France and Thomas Jefferson for trying to weaken the federal government. Indeed, at the Constitutional Convention, Hamilton had proposed a federal government so strong that it would have appointed the states' governors too. Now, 13 years later, Hamilton hoped that each of South Carolina's eight electors would cast their first votes for their native son, Charles C. Pinckney, who was Adams's running mate, while Jefferson and Adams might divide the electors' second votes between them. If this happened, Pinckney would outpoll Jefferson and Adams by three electoral votes and win the presidency. Amid the many meetings and deals taking place in South Carolina's new capital city, Columbia, this was a real possibility.

South Carolina's inland representatives were disciplined, however, and maintained their small Republican majority in the legislature. Originally the Republicans intended to cast eight electoral votes for Jefferson, seven for Burr, and one for someone else, perhaps Pinckney, to ensure that Jefferson was elected president and Burr was elected vice president. But because of the widespread fear that Hamilton's favored candidate, Pinckney, might surprise everyone and outpoll Burr, no one voted for Pinckney, and Burr received votes from all eight of South Carolina's electors.

The nation's final electoral vote was, therefore, Jefferson 73, Burr 73, Adams 65, Pinckney 64, and John Jay 1. The vote for president was a tie.

Federalists were jubilant. Under the Constitution then, a tie vote would be decided by the House of Representatives, which could only choose between the top two candidates: Jefferson and Burr. But in a slower horse-drawn age, the newly elected US House of Representatives, with its massive Jeffersonian majority, would not meet for many months. The election would therefore be decided by the lame-duck House that was still in session, where the Federalists held a slim a 53–51 majority. And the House's balloting, under Article II of the Constitution, would be one-state-one-vote.

"Everybody is aware of that defect in the constitution," Hamilton foresaw in 1789, "which renders it possible that the man intended for vice president may, in fact, turn up president." Eleven years later, Jefferson was miffed. He had made a mistake, he wrote a friend, because "I never once asked whether arrangements had been made [to hold back a vote for Burr] nor did I doubt till lately that such [arrangements] had been made."

1800

☐ **Democratic-Republican (Jefferson)**
▨ **Federalist (Adams)**
▨ **Territories**

ELECTORAL VOTES

Jefferson	73
Burr	73
Adams	65
Pinckney	64
Jay	1

Possession of Spain

James Madison blamed Burr for the fiasco, suspecting, without any evidence, that Burr's friends had told New York's electors that an elector in Virginia was withholding a vote, and Virginia's electors that someone in New York was withholding a vote.

In the congressional elections, the Republicans had routed the Federalists, winning 67 of the new House's 106 seats, including a third of the seats in Federalist New England, because most Americans wanted lower taxes, a repeal of the Sedition Act, and a government that was more sympathetic to working people than to the elite. Indeed, considering the strength of this Republican tide, President Adams did remarkably well. Were it not for the early Constitution's infamous "⅗" rule that allowed southern states to count three-fifths of their slaves as population for the purpose of congressional and electoral apportionment, Adams would have narrowly beaten Jefferson by an electoral vote of 70 to 68.

Instead, Adams's term would end on March 4, 1801. (Inauguration Day did not move from March 4 to January 20 until 1937.) But who would be the next president? The Federalists were overjoyed at having a second chance to deny Jefferson the presidency, because Jefferson's "atheism" worried them more than Burr's questionable character. At least Burr "is not a *declared* infidel," said Massachusetts's Theodore Sedgwick, the Speaker of the nation's lame-duck House, and "he would not be able to administer the government without the aid of the Federalists." The Federalists also preferred Burr because he was a New York lawyer with administrative ability, while Jefferson was a southern planter who wanted smaller government.

Alexander Hamilton, who had known Burr in New York for years, was aghast at the prospect of a Burr presidency. He spent the Christmas holidays writing letter after letter to the Federalists in Congress, including one to Harrison Gray Otis of Massachusetts:

> *Mr. Jefferson, though too revolutionary in his notions, is yet a lover of liberty . . . Mr. Burr loves nothing but himself . . . and will be content with nothing short of permanent power in his own hands.*

Hamilton also warned the Federalists that Burr would start a war to increase his power.

Even Jefferson confessed years later that he had always looked upon Burr as "a crooked gun," a stunning admission considering that Jefferson had agreed to Burr's being just one heartbeat away from the presidency.

During the winter of 1800–1801, Burr was in Albany serving as a New York state assemblyman. As if to prove Hamilton's charge that he was power hungry, Burr refused to do the one thing that would have ended the national crisis quickly: publicly declare that he would refuse the presidency even if the Federalists elected him. Instead, Burr said that while he wouldn't actively seek the presidency, neither would he reject the office if the House picked him rather than Jefferson.

At noon on Wednesday, February 11, 1801, Congress finally convened to choose a president. At the time, the nation had 16 states; the votes of a majority (i.e., nine states' congressional delegations) were required to win. Eight states stretching from New York to Georgia were for Jefferson, and six states (four in New England, plus Delaware and South Carolina) were for Burr. Two more states, Vermont and Maryland, were deadlocked because their delegations were evenly divided and therefore could not vote.

Each congressman's vote was crucial. A single extra vote from Maryland or Vermont would have tipped the presidency to Jefferson. But three additional votes from any of five different states would have tipped the presidency to Burr. One congressman, Joseph Nicholson of Maryland, had pneumonia, yet his slaves carried him on a cot through two miles of snow and icy wind to the partially completed Capitol building so that he could cast his vote.

The afternoon began pleasantly with a joint session of the House and Senate. Jefferson, who was still the nation's vice president and the Senate's presiding officer, read aloud the electoral votes cast by each of the 16 states and announced the final total: 73 electoral votes for himself, and 73 votes for Burr. After this formality, Jefferson and all the US senators left the room so that the House of Representatives could start voting for president.

For 14 ballots, the vote was the same: 8 states for Jefferson, 6 states for Burr, and Vermont and Maryland deadlocked and unable to vote. The congressmen adjourned for dinner, then voted again every hour, all through the night. At dawn, after 27 ballots, the vote was still the same: 8 states for Jefferson and 6 states for Burr. (If the congressmen could have voted individually rather than by state, the total would have been Jefferson 55, Burr 49, because four Federalists were voting for Jefferson.)

Six more ballots on Thursday, Friday, and Saturday changed nothing, and finally the frustrated congressmen took Sunday off. By Monday, February 16, when they began voting again, Inauguration Day, March 4, was only 16 days away.

Some Federalists wanted Congress to pass a law declaring that if there were not a duly elected president or vice president by the time President Adams's term expired, then either Secretary of State John Marshall or Chief Justice John Jay (both Federalists) would become president.

"If the union could be broken, that would do it," wrote James Monroe, who was then the governor of Virginia. Together, he and the governor of Pennsylvania, Thomas McKean, got ready to send more than 20,000 troops to Washington to arrest any congressman who voted for anyone other than Jefferson or Burr as president. Albert Gallatin, the Republican majority leader in the House of Representatives, took an even harder line.

A thousand men from Maryland were poised to march to Washington, Gallatin threatened, "for the purpose of putting to death [any] usurping pretended President."

By coincidence, Jefferson walked past President Adams on Pennsylvania Avenue one day and expressed his alarm at the prospect of the Federalists electing Burr. "Sir," Adams said to Jefferson, "the event of the election is within your own power." Adams was referring to a deal that Alexander Hamilton and several other Federalists had proposed to Jefferson. These Federalists would support Jefferson's election as president if he would promise not to renounce the national debt, disband the navy, or ally with France. Jefferson refused. "I will not come into the government by capitulation," he replied, "but in perfect freedom to follow the dictates of my own judgment."

The key man in Congress now was Delaware's lone representative, James Bayard, a Federalist lawyer known for dressing stylishly. Hamilton wrote him nearly weekly about the defects of Burr's character, and Bayard finally decided that if Burr could not win, he would vote for Jefferson rather than risk the breakup of the nation. Two more Federalist congressmen, one from Maryland and another from Vermont, secretly agreed to follow Bayard's lead.

Samuel Smith, a Republican congressman from Maryland, served as an intermediary between Bayard and Jefferson. Smith talked to Jefferson about the issues, but never told him that he was also talking to Bayard. Jefferson assured Smith that he would not repudiate the debt, disband the navy, or abandon neutrality. Smith relayed these assurances to Bayard, but cautioned that they were Jefferson's opinions, not his promises. Bayard was satisfied. On Monday he told the other Federalist congressmen that he would vote for Jefferson, which would give Jefferson nine states and the presidency. "Deserter!" one Federalist shouted, but Bayard was undeterred.

On Tuesday, February 17, 1801, on the 36th ballot, the two congressmen from Maryland and Vermont followed Bayard's lead and abstained, which meant these two states were no longer evenly divided and deadlocked, but now had a majority of congressmen who could vote for Jefferson, which gave Jefferson 10 states and the presidency. Bayard did not

1801

THE FINAL VOTE IN THE HOUSE

Jefferson	☐	10 states
Burr	▨	4 states
Not voting	▩	2 states
Territories	▨	

Possession
of Spain

have to vote for Jefferson himself. It was enough that he abstained, as did some other Federalist congressmen from South Carolina. The final vote was therefore 10 states for Jefferson and 4 states (all from New England) for Burr, with 2 states, Delaware and South Carolina, casting blank ballots. Thomas Jefferson was finally elected America's third president.

As the news of Jefferson's election spread by horseback, joyful Republicans lit bonfires and fired cannons, and offered toasts to Jefferson and to "the Tree of Liberty, moistened by the tears of Aristocracy." In Philadelphia, church bells rang, causing one Federalist woman to sneer that the bells were "pealing for an infidel."

President Adams had just moved into the newly finished White House the previous November, when some of its walls were still wet with paint. On his second day there, he had written his wife, Abigail, who was still in Philadelphia, "May none but honest and wise men ever rule under this roof," a sentence that was later carved over the fireplace in the White House's State Dining Room.

Now, only four months later, Adams had to leave. Although defeated in his bid for reelection, Adams was proud of his presidency. He left the nation, he wrote a friend, "with its coffers full," "its commerce flourishing," and with "fair prospects of peace with all the world." Abigail was less sanguine. "The golden age is past," she wrote a companion. "God grant that it may not be succeeded by an age of terror."

No tradition yet existed of an outgoing president attending the swearing in of his successor, so on Inauguration Day, March 4, 1801, John Adams left the White House by public stagecoach at four o'clock in the morning. The passengers needed to leave that early to reach Baltimore by dinnertime.

A few hours later, President-Elect Thomas Jefferson, a guest that morning at Conrad & McMunn's Boarding House, ate breakfast at a communal table and declined an offer to sit in a warmer chair closer to the fire. When he finished eating, Jefferson walked to the Capitol to give his inaugural address. "We are all Republicans, we are all Federalists," he told the crowd, meaning that every American wants both individual freedom and an effective government. Jefferson promised to honor both the national debt and the treaty of neutrality, which pleased Hamilton greatly. But Jefferson reduced the size of the navy, and he pardoned everyone convicted under the Sedition Act.

Without question, Jefferson owed his victory in the House of Representatives to Alexander Hamilton's many letters to Federalist congressmen denouncing Aaron Burr. Burr served four years as Jefferson's vice president, but his career never recovered from the mistrust that he had aroused in Jefferson and every other Republican when he refused to stop the attempt by the Federalists to elect him president.

During the entire campaign the very thought of Jefferson as president had horrified the Federalists, but when the dreaded moment of Jefferson's inauguration on March 4 finally came, they accepted his ascension with remarkable calm. For the first time in history, one political party peacefully transferred power to another. From Jefferson's point of view, power had shifted from a party that distrusted the people to a party that had confidence in them.

Americans had set a precedent: Opposing parties would take turns governing. There would be no assassinations, no military coups, no suspensions of the Constitution. Neither side would crush the other. The losing party would simply wait for the next election. "What a lesson to America and the world," Madison exulted a week before Jefferson's inauguration.

~

Americans breathed a sigh of relief that the electoral crisis had passed, then shuddered as they realized that the voting method that had caused the crisis was still a part of the Constitution. As the next presidential election in 1804 grew closer, both Republicans and Federalists were determined to separate the electoral votes for president and vice president. The very reason that electors cast two votes for president—to ensure that they would vote for someone worthwhile from another state—no longer made sense. Campaigns were already national in character, and electoral votes for out-of-state candidates had become the norm.

In December 1803 both the House and the Senate approved a new 12th Amendment to the Constitution that gave electors just one vote for president and another vote for vice president. The 1804 election was less than a year away, but few people wanted the old system of electors having two votes for president to continue, so 14 state legislatures, from both the North and the South, ratified the 12th Amendment in the next six months, just in time for the 1804 election. Since then, candidates for president and vice president have continued to run together as a ticket, but never again has there been any confusion about which office an elector was voting for.

The 12th Amendment also reaffirmed the strange provision in Article II of the Constitution that if no presidential candidate wins a majority of the electoral vote, the House of Representatives shall decide the election on a one-state-one-vote basis. But the new amendment declared that the House would have to choose a president from among the top three (rather than the top five) electoral-vote winners. In 1801, of course, it was hard enough for the House of Representatives to choose a president when there was a tie between only two candidates. If an election should move to the House again when there are *three* presidential candidates, the chance of having another long, multi-ballot fiasco in Congress is substantial.

In the two centuries since the 12th Amendment was ratified, the world has industrialized, communication has become instant, and Blacks, women, and 18-year-olds have won the right to vote. Yet the constitutional provisions that govern our electoral system have not changed at all. Senators and representatives have proposed hundreds of constitutional amendments to try to improve the way we elect a president, but the last one to be passed and ratified, the 12th, predates the telegraph, the bicycle, and even the cylindrical bullet.

CHAPTER 6

The House Decides Again

John Quincy Adams vs. Andrew Jackson (1824)

THE 1800 ELECTION WENT TO THE HOUSE OF REPRESENTATIVES BECAUSE the electoral vote between Thomas Jefferson and Aaron Burr had been a tie. Today a 269–269 tie in the electoral vote is highly unlikely, although it would have happened in 2000 if Al Gore had won the close states of New Hampshire and Tennessee, which narrowly went for George W. Bush, and Bush had taken the even closer states of Iowa and New Mexico, which narrowly went for Gore.

What is much more likely to happen again is what took place in 1824, when four prominent men ran for president and no one won a majority of the electoral vote, which shifted the election to the House of Representatives. All we need are strong Tea Party and Green Party candidates in the same year.

The reason four candidates ran in 1824 is that there had been an interruption in the two-party system. The Federalist Party, which had opposed the War of 1812, was defunct, but the Whig Party had not yet formed. In 1824 almost everyone called himself a "Democratic-Republican," including each of the four presidential candidates: Secretary of State John Quincy Adams, General Andrew Jackson, Speaker of the House Henry Clay, and Secretary of the Treasury William Crawford. Because the issues that divided them were small, the 1824 vote was more like a party primary than a general election.

The most accomplished candidate was John Quincy Adams, who was finishing his second term as James Monroe's secretary of state. Adams had successfully negotiated America's purchase of Florida from Spain, delineated a border with Britain between what is now Canada and North Dakota, and agreed to another border on the Pacific coast between what was then the Spanish territory of California and the American territory of Oregon. Most important, Adams had conceived the Monroe Doctrine that prevented Europe from interfering with Latin America's newly independent nations. With the exception of Harry Truman's secretaries of state, George Marshall and Dean Acheson, Adams was probably the greatest secretary of state in history.

John Quincy's father, John Adams, expected no less. "If you do not rise to the head not only of your profession, but of your country," Adams wrote his son in the 1790s, "it will be owing to your own *Laziness, Slovenliness,* and *Obstinacy.*" His mother, Abigail Adams, wrote even more critical letters, telling him to work hard, dress neatly, and avoid temptation. Not surprisingly, Adams grew up to be Spartan, self-critical, and dour. He was also short, bald, and had a shrill voice.

John Quincy Adams was born near Boston in 1767, when his father was already a successful lawyer. When he was nearly eight, his mother led him by the hand up Bunker Hill so that he could see the Massachusetts militiamen fight the British redcoats and better appreciate the price of freedom. Three years later John Adams, now a diplomat for the newly formed United States, took his son to Paris. John Quincy quickly became fluent in French, Greek, and Latin, and studied German, mathematics, and fencing too. He also developed a lifelong love for French theater and opera.

By the time Adams was 15, he was reading Cicero, Pope, Hume, and Voltaire, and astonishing adults with his superb conversation. At 16 he became his father's private secretary when the elder Adams returned to Paris to negotiate the peace treaty with Britain that ended the Revolutionary War. John Quincy spent many evenings in the city with Thomas Jefferson, who greatly enjoyed talking with the brilliant teenager about science, history, and literature.

Returning to Boston and graduating second in his class at Harvard, Adams pleased his parents by studying law even though it never interested him. He wanted to marry a beautiful and intelligent 16-year-old, Mary Frazier, who was probably the love of his life, but both sets of parents were against the match because Adams, still a student in his early 20s, did not yet have an income.

As a young lawyer, Adams wrote articles in 1793 that defended President Washington's policy of neutrality between Britain and France, and one year later Washington appointed Adams, only 27, to be US Minister to the Netherlands. At 30, Adams married Louisa Johnson, the daughter an American diplomat in London. When Abigail expressed some doubts about Louisa during their courtship, Adams wrote his mother that if he waited until she approved of a young woman, he "would certainly be doomed to perpetual celibacy." Chastened, Abigail wrote back that she would treat Louisa as a daughter.

In 1797 the new president, John Adams, chose his newlywed son to be the US Minister to Prussia, and greatly enjoyed reading his son's long letters from Berlin about European war and politics. Four years later, when Jefferson became president, young Adams returned to Boston to practice law. The Federalists there asked him to run for the state senate in 1802, and a year later the Massachusetts state legislature elected him to the US Senate.

Even when Adams was a US senator, his mother still wrote nagging letters. "I hope you never appear in [the] Senate with a beard two days old," she wrote. She also cautioned her son to brush his coat and eat more.

In Congress, Adams was the only Federalist to support the Louisiana Purchase, and the only Federalist to support President Jefferson's 1807 ban on trade with Britain, which Jefferson reluctantly imposed because the British navy, fighting Napoleon, was seizing American merchant ships that were headed for France. Federalists in the Massachusetts legislature were disgusted with Adams's support for Jefferson's trade embargo, and chose Adams's successor in the Senate a full year and a half before his senate term was due to expire. Adams took the hint, resigned from the Senate, and ended his affiliation with the Federalists. Within a decade, the Federalist Party was gone, but Adams's career kept advancing.

When James Madison became president in 1809, he appointed Adams Minister to Russia. In St. Petersburg, Adams became good friends with Czar Alexander I, probably because the czar needed a confidant who was neutral in European affairs. They took long walks together, speaking in French about the rise of Napoleon, Russian politics, and life in the United States, a country that fascinated the young monarch.

Three years later, at nearly the same time that Napoleon invaded Russia, the United States and Britain began fighting the War of 1812. By 1814, with Napoleon in retreat from Russia and Washington, DC, in flames, Britain's political and military position had strengthened, so President Madison sent five men to the Belgian city of Ghent to try to negotiate peace with the British. Adams led the delegation, which also included Kentucky Congressman Henry Clay (who would run for president against Adams 10 years later) and Delaware Senator James Bayard, the man who had prevented a civil war in 1801 when he stopped voting for Aaron Burr after 35 ballots in the House of Representatives.

In Ghent, Adams went to bed early while Clay played cards until four in the morning. Yet the two men worked well together, and the British dropped their demand for a buffer state of Indian tribes west of the Appalachian Mountains. The United States and Great Britain signed a peace treaty on Christmas Eve 1814, with every border between British and American territory exactly the same as it had been before the war. The news of the peace, however, did not reach America until after Andrew Jackson had defeated the British at the Battle of New Orleans two weeks later.

Adams served two years as US Minister to Britain, then in 1817 a new president, James Monroe, asked Adams to be his secretary of state. General Jackson, America's war hero, praised Monroe's choice, writing the new president, "You have made the best selection to fill the Department of State that could be made."

——◆——

Andrew Jackson, like John Quincy Adams, was born in 1767 and ran for president in 1824, but his boyhood could not have been more different. Adams, the son of a president, was educated in Europe and at Harvard.

By contrast, Jackson was the son of a linen weaver from Northern Ireland who had moved to South Carolina to clear a farm in the woods before he died in a tree-cutting accident just before Jackson was born. Jackson, unlike Adams, had only a few years of schooling (his spelling would always be dreadful) but grew up to be tall, handsome, and charismatic.

When he was 14, Jackson and his brother were captured by British troops during the Revolutionary War. A British officer ordered Jackson to shine his boots, but Jackson refused. Enraged, the redcoat swung his sword and slashed Jackson's face, leaving him with both a scar and a life-long hostility toward Britain.

Jackson's mother arranged a prisoner exchange to win her sons' freedom, but Jackson's brother died of smallpox that he had caught in prison, and his mother soon died of cholera after she helped to nurse some wounded American soldiers. Jackson was suddenly an orphan with no siblings.

At 15, Jackson inherited several hundred dollars from an Irish grand-father, which he squandered on clothes, pistols, women, and a fast horse. After the money ran out, Jackson moved to Salisbury, North Carolina. Still in his teens, he spent his days reading law and clerking for an attorney, and his nights carousing with friends. One neighbor remembered Jackson as "the most roaring, rollicking, game-cocking, horse-racing, card-playing, mischievous fellow that ever lived."

By the time he was 20, Jackson was licensed to practice law in North Carolina. A year later he moved to Nashville, which was then a village of only 200 people and still a part of North Carolina, because a friend had hired him to be a prosecutor there. Jackson lived in a boardinghouse and fell in love with the innkeeper's daughter, Rachel Donelson. But through confusion or carelessness, they married before her divorce from her previous husband was final. The unfortunate timing would later lead to several duels, and during the bitter presidential election of 1828, to pamphlets that charged Jackson's wife with bigamy.

In 1794 Jackson became attorney general for the new Tennessee Territory's Central District. By then he owned several hundred acres of land and 16 slaves. When Tennessee became a state two years later, voters elected Jackson to Congress and then, in 1797, to the US Senate.

But Jackson made little impression in Philadelphia, which was still the nation's capital, because he struck most of his colleagues as an uncouth backwoodsman.

Returning to Tennessee, Jackson served as a circuit judge, traveling from one county courthouse to another. James Parton, a 19th-century biographer, described Jackson's judicial decisions as "short, untechnical, unlearned, sometimes ungrammatical, and generally right." Jackson also became a major general in Tennessee's militia in 1802.

In 1806 a quarrel over a horse race grew heated after Charles Dickinson paid for a newspaper ad that called Jackson a scoundrel and a coward. Jackson challenged Dickinson to a duel, but because Dickinson was one of the best marksmen in Tennessee, Jackson decided in advance to let Dickinson fire first so that he could then take all the time he needed to aim carefully and fire back. Jackson also wore a big overcoat to hide the contours of his thin body. The strategy worked. Dickinson shot Jackson in the chest, but the wound was not fatal, and Jackson's return shot was.

Jackson's hot temper led to a dozen duels during his lifetime, but the duel with Dickinson was the only one where someone died. In Jackson's first duel, for example, both men, after their anger cooled, agreed beforehand to deliberately miss and then shake hands. When Jackson killed Dickinson, which under the South's code duello he had a right to do, it was because he had already forgiven Dickinson once for having called his wife a bigamist.

During the War of 1812, Jackson fought tribes in Alabama. The British had encouraged Native Americans to attack US villages, and in 1813 Creek warriors massacred more than 250 American men, women, and children at Fort Mims in southern Alabama. In retaliation, Jackson led 4,000 volunteers south from Nashville and surrounded the largest Creek fortress at Horseshoe Bend, northeast of Montgomery, where his men killed nearly 900 Creeks while losing only 47 men themselves. Jackson had always regarded the Creek tribe's land as a senseless barrier to white settlement. Now he forced the defeated Creeks to sign a treaty giving up what today is 60% of Alabama and 20% of Georgia.

Before and during this battle, Jackson marched with his men and shared their hardships. Admiring his toughness, Jackson's men, including a young officer named Sam Houston, began calling him "Old Hickory," because hickory is a particularly hard wood. After the battle, Jackson adopted a baby Creek boy whose parents had been killed. He called him Lyncoya and raised him as a son until the boy died of illness at 16, just before Jackson was elected president.

In the autumn of 1814, Americans were alarmed to learn that the British had launched 60 ships from Jamaica carrying 10,000 soldiers to attack New Orleans. Britain had never recognized Spain's grant of the Louisiana territory to France in 1800, so the British claimed that America's purchase of the territory from France in 1803 was also illegitimate, arguing that Louisiana had never been France's colony to sell in the first place. Americans were afraid that if British troops captured New Orleans and marched north, they might try to take the rest of the vast Louisiana Purchase away from the United States too.

Jackson rushed to New Orleans with 700 men, declared martial law, and built long riverside barricades of sugar barrels, dried mud, and cotton bales. Over the objections of Louisiana's slaveholders, he also formed two battalions of free Black soldiers, most of whom received some land after the battle. Four thousand more troops arrived from Kentucky, Tennessee, and Mississippi, but the British soldiers still outnumbered the Americans two to one, and they were battle-hardened veterans who had successfully fought Napoleon.

Fortunately for the Americans, only some of the British troops sent to cross the Mississippi and seize US fortifications were actually able to take barges across the river, and 500 of those who did landed too far south to take part in any fighting. More important, Jackson rushed 20 artillery crews to the battlefront to fire cannons at the British from only 500 yards away, and the nearly 4,000 Kentucky and Tennessee riflemen who crouched behind the barricades were excellent marksmen.

At dawn on January 8, 1815, while some Scottish soldiers played the bagpipes, Jackson's men massacred the British. When the two-hour battle was over, the Americans had killed nearly 300 British troops and wounded more than 1,500, while suffering only 13 dead and 39 wounded. Within days, the defeated British reboarded their ships and sailed back to Jamaica.

Andrew Jackson immediately became the country's biggest hero since George Washington. Americans everywhere exulted in their frontiersmen's victory over the British veterans, and President James Madison put General Jackson in command of the southern half of the US army.

Three years later a new president, James Monroe, asked Jackson to stop the attacks by Seminole warriors on American villages in Georgia and Alabama. The raids were launched from Florida, which was still a Spanish colony. In the spring of 1818, Jackson led 3,000 men southward; burned a Seminole fort; and captured, tried, and executed two British agents who had been arming the Seminoles. He also seized the town of Pensacola, which effectively established American control over western Florida.

The secretary of the treasury, William Crawford, who would run for president against Jackson only six years later, said that Jackson had grossly exceeded President Monroe's instructions, and called for Jackson's censure and the return of western Florida to Spain. The secretary of war, John Calhoun, agreed.

Only John Quincy Adams, President Monroe's secretary of state, defended Jackson. Adams said that Jackson's Florida campaign was a defensive action, and that Spain had brought this invasion on itself by failing to restrain the Seminoles. Monroe agreed with Adams and declined to reprimand Jackson. A year later Adams completed the purchase of Florida from Spain for $5 million, and in 1821 Jackson became the territory's first American governor. (Jacksonville, Florida, is named for the general.)

The 1819 treaty between the United States and Spain set the border between Texas and Louisiana along the Sabine and Red Rivers. On the Pacific, it also made the 42nd parallel of latitude the boundary between California, which still belonged to Spain, and Oregon, which the United States jointly shared with Britain. Once Spain gave up its own claim to Oregon, the United States, for the first time, legally stretched to the Pacific.

The Speaker of the House, Henry Clay, who would also run for president in 1824, was appalled by Jackson's conquest of Florida, calling it "insubordination—a triumph of the military over the civilian authority." Clay wanted to be the first president from a western state. He not only saw Jackson as a rival, but truly believed that electing an army general as president was the first step toward military dictatorship.

A brilliant lawyer from Kentucky, Clay was born a few miles north of Richmond, Virginia, in 1777. As a teenager, he worked as a law clerk for George Wythe, a signer of the Declaration of Independence who long ago had also mentored the young Thomas Jefferson. Clay had the full use of Wythe's large library, and read works of history and literature as well as the law. But Richmond had many attorneys, so at 21 Clay moved west to practice law in Lexington, Kentucky.

The new state's many cases of overlapping land claims made Clay rich, but he also became known for his pleasing voice, wide learning, and the concentrated personal attention that he gave to nearly everyone. In 1811 Kentucky's voters sent Clay to the US House of Representatives, and because half of its members that year were new, seniority counted for little. The freshman congressmen banded together and elected Clay, only 34, Speaker of the House.

Clay was a much stronger leader than previous Speakers had been, and helped levy taxes on European imports to pay for roads, bridges, and canals. He also brokered the Missouri Compromise of 1820, the law that admitted Maine as a free state and Missouri as a slave state, and drew a line of latitude (36 degrees 30 minutes, between what would later be the Texas and Oklahoma panhandles) to separate free territory from slave territory in the future.

The fourth candidate for president in 1824 was William Crawford, President Monroe's secretary of the treasury. A Virginian who moved to Georgia at 11, Crawford spent his teens plowing his father's fields, but also learned to read Cicero and Virgil in Latin. Handsome, cheerful, and six-feet-three, Crawford became a lawyer, a US senator, the Minister to France, and President Madison's secretary of war. Many congressmen wanted Crawford to run for president in 1816, but Crawford finally decided to support James Monroe instead. President Monroe returned the favor by appointing Crawford secretary of the treasury, a position Crawford held during both of Monroe's terms.

Crawford's persistent efforts to reduce government spending made him a favorite of the Democratic-Republicans in Congress, and also of Thomas Jefferson, who thought Jackson was a hothead and that Adams, although brilliant, would make the federal government too strong. Unfortunately, Crawford suffered a massive stroke in September 1823 that left him paralyzed, almost blind, and nearly speechless. Sixty-two congressmen backed him for president anyway, but their endorsements no longer mattered much. By then, the people rather than their state legislators voted for presidential electors in two-thirds of the states, whether they owned property or not, and most voters did not care who the elites in Washington endorsed.

A fifth man also briefly ran for president, John Calhoun of South Carolina, President Monroe's secretary of war. The Yale graduate and former congressman had not yet become the South's leading defender of slavery, and in 1824 his ambition was to win the presidency by taking not only the South but also Pennsylvania. But when it became clear that most Pennsylvanians preferred Andrew Jackson, Calhoun ended his pursuit of the presidency and announced his willingness to run as a vice presidential running mate under either Adams or Jackson. Both men accepted Calhoun's offer, so while the vote for president in 1824 was divided among four candidates, the vote for vice president was a landslide, with Calhoun winning 182 of the nation's 260 electoral votes. Calhoun was vice president for eight years, serving under John Quincy Adams and serving under Jackson during his first term.

In the early 1820s most Americans were still recovering from the financial panic of 1819, and there was a new, rather sour feeling that presidents should no longer be succeeded by their secretaries of state. In 1822 Tennessee's state legislature endorsed Andrew Jackson for president, and support for the war hero quickly spread to other states, including South Carolina and Pennsylvania. Even John Quincy Adams said that he would prefer Jackson as president to Clay, Crawford, or Calhoun.

Voting in 1824 began in the spring, when the legislatures of six states picked their presidential electors. New York and Vermont supported Adams, South Carolina and Louisiana endorsed Jackson, and Georgia and Delaware went for William Crawford. The early electoral vote was Adams 36, Crawford 16, Jackson 15, and Clay 4. In the autumn, ordinary people would choose another 190 electors, and for many it would be the first time that they had ever voted in a presidential election.

While the candidates themselves did not campaign, their supporters made up for this restraint with thousands of pamphlets and newspaper editorials. Because all four candidates in 1824 belonged to the same party, however, and because everyone still liked the outgoing president, James Monroe, the tone of the campaign was unusually genteel.

By the time the last state voted, the popular vote across the nation was Jackson 41%, Adams 31%, Clay 13%, and Crawford 11%, and the electoral vote was Jackson 99, Adams 84, Crawford 41, and Clay 37. Each candidate did well in his own part of the country: Jackson in the South, Adams in the Northeast, Clay along the Ohio River, and Crawford in his home states of Georgia and Virginia. But Jackson not only won his own region, he also took Pennsylvania, New Jersey, Illinois, and Indiana.

Because no one won a majority of the electoral vote, the election shifted to the House of Representatives, which would cast its ballots according to the quirky one-state-one-vote arrangement. Louis McLane, Delaware's lone congressman, was about to have a vote equal to that of all 34 congressmen from New York. And because the Constitution's 12th Amendment limits the House's choice of presidential candidates to the top *three* winners of the electoral vote, Henry Clay, who finished fourth, was eliminated from the contest even though he had won slightly more popular votes than William Crawford.

Ironically, the House overwhelmingly reelected Clay as its Speaker. Had he finished third rather than fourth in the electoral vote, the House would surely have elected Clay president. Instead, although he was out of the race himself, Clay was in an extraordinary position to influence the House's vote for president.

Clay leaned strongly toward Adams. He did not particularly like him, but Crawford was an invalid, and Clay thought Jackson unfit. In a letter

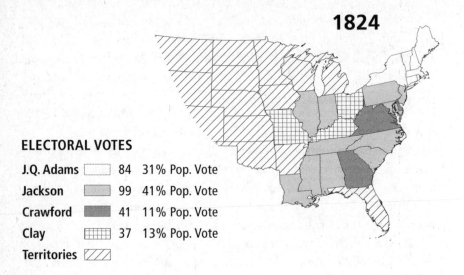

1824

ELECTORAL VOTES

J.Q. Adams		84	31% Pop. Vote
Jackson		99	41% Pop. Vote
Crawford		41	11% Pop. Vote
Clay		37	13% Pop. Vote
Territories			

to a friend, Clay wrote, "I cannot believe that killing 2,500 Englishmen at N. Orleans qualifies for the various, difficult, and complicated duties of the Chief Magistracy." As word spread about Clay's thinking, the legislature of Kentucky, Clay's home state, formally instructed its congressmen to vote for Jackson. But the congressmen, who were good friends of Clay, said that they would ignore their state's instructions, which legally they were free to do.

On Sunday evening, January 9, 1825, Henry Clay visited John Quincy Adams at his home in Washington for three hours. Clay wanted to make sure that Adams favored tariffs on imports to pay for roads and canals, and that he approved of using the Second National Bank of the United States to make the loans to finance them. Adams had already publicly supported these positions, and by confirming them in person he won Clay's support.

In Congress, Clay lobbied hard for Adams, securing the backing of representatives from Ohio, Kentucky, and Missouri, the states that Clay had won in the presidential election. He also encouraged Daniel Cook, the lone congressman from Illinois, to follow his conscience and vote for Adams, even though Jackson had won the state by a narrow margin. Clay also won over congressmen from Maryland and Louisiana, states that had also gone for Jackson.

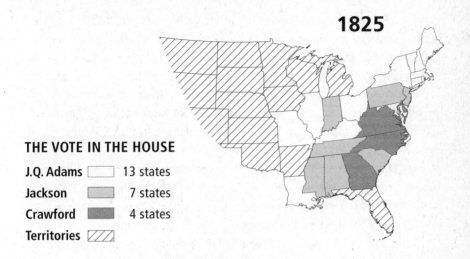

1825

THE VOTE IN THE HOUSE

J.Q. Adams ☐ 13 states

Jackson ▨ 7 states

Crawford ▪ 4 states

Territories ▨

Because there were 24 states in 1825, a candidate needed the vote of 13 states' congressional delegations to win. Adams had the solid support of 9 states, Jackson 7, and Crawford 2. Of the remaining six states, Crawford picked up North Carolina and Delaware even though Jackson had won both of these states in the presidential election, and Adams won the support of three more states that Jackson had won: Maryland, Illinois, and Louisiana.

Jackson's supporters were particularly angry that Louisiana's congressmen voted for Adams. Didn't they remember that Jackson had saved their state from British conquest only nine years before? "Louisianeans! Degraded, Ungrateful Men!! to vote against you!" one friend wrote Jackson, "You!! who under God, they are indebted for their soil! The Protector of the Chastity of their wives and daughters!!"*

The day before the House's big vote, the tally stood at 12 states for Adams, 7 for Jackson, and 4 for Crawford. Adams was one state short of victory because New York could not cast a vote. Its 34 congressmen were deadlocked: 17 were for Adams, 15 favored Crawford, and 2 were for Jackson. No one had a majority of New York's congressmen.

---

* Lynn Hudson Parsons, *The Birth of Modern Politics, Andrew Jackson, John Quincy Adams, and the Election of 1828* (Oxford: Oxford University Press, 2009), 105.

One New Yorker was wavering, however: Congressman Stephen Van Rensselaer. The owner of a vast estate along the Hudson River, the easygoing Van Rensselaer had promised Senator Martin Van Buren that he would vote for William Crawford for president. But Henry Clay and his fellow congressman, Daniel Webster, invited Van Rensselaer into Clay's private study and took turns for more than an hour warning Van Rensselaer about the chaos ahead if Congress failed to elect a president. President Monroe was leaving office in only three weeks, they reminded Van Rensselaer, and without a new president (or worse, with the invalid Crawford as president), the new vice president, South Carolina's John Calhoun, could become acting president. Completely bewildered, Van Rensselaer left Clay's office in tears, not knowing how he would vote.

On February 9, 1825, during a heavy snowfall, Congress finally convened to choose a president. Speaker Clay began the session by declaring that while John Calhoun had won a majority of the electoral votes for vice president, no one had won a majority of the electoral votes for president. At this point the US senators left the chamber to let the members of the House begin voting.

In the end, Congressman Van Rensselaer broke the promise he made to Senator Van Buren to vote for Crawford and voted for Adams instead, so by a vote of 18 (for Adams) to 14 (for Crawford) to 2 (for Jackson), New York's congressional delegation was able to vote as a bloc for Adams. This gave Adams 13 states to Jackson's 7 and Crawford's 4. On the first ballot, the House of Representatives elected John Quincy Adams the sixth president of the United States.

When the elder John Adams heard the good news about his son, he wept with joy. His only regret, he said, was that his wife, Abigail, who had died in 1818, had not lived to hear the news too. Andrew Jackson, however, was shocked by the House's vote. Jackson had won not only the most popular votes in 1824, but the most electoral votes too, so he had expected the House to confirm what he believed was the will of the people. To this day, no one else has ever won the most electoral votes and lost the presidency.

Less than a week after the House's vote, President-Elect Adams appointed Henry Clay as his secretary of state. Clay was a natural candidate for the post because he had diplomatic experience, agreed with Adams on the issues, and offered geographical balance to the New England–led administration. But it was a disastrous choice. Even if there was never any direct agreement between Adams and Clay about the appointment, it looked as if the two men had struck an insider's deal, with Clay supporting Adams during the vote for president in the House in return for Adams offering the State Department to Clay. One politician mocked Adams as "our *Clay President.*"

Jackson's supporters called Adams's choice of Clay a "corrupt bargain." There was nothing illegal or unconstitutional about the appointment, but the two words stuck to Adams for the rest of his presidency, and to Clay for the rest of his life. Jackson had never forgiven Clay for calling him a power-hungry "military chieftain" during his battles against the Seminoles in Florida. Now, Jackson wrote with venom, "the Judas of the West [Clay] has closed the contract and will receive his thirty pieces of silver. His end will be the same." Jackson was prescient. Clay never did win the presidency, losing to Jackson in a landslide in 1832 and to Jackson's protégé, James Knox Polk, in a closer race in 1844.

Jackson's many supporters throughout the nation started a new campaign for the presidency almost as soon as Adams was inaugurated. They formed a vast network of party workers that reached the smallest farms and poorest slums, and published newspapers that mocked Adams as an effeminate aristocrat.

Their efforts paid off. In the congressional elections of 1826, the voters kicked out nearly all the congressmen from the South and West who had voted for Adams for president the year before, and gave pro-Jackson congressmen solid majorities in both the House and the Senate. It was the first time that opponents of a sitting president had won control of both houses of Congress.

The election of 1828, when Jackson ran for president against Adams again, was the nastiest campaign in American history. The pro-Jackson *New Hampshire Patriot* said that Adams had pimped for Czar Alexander I when he was Minister to Russia, while a pro-Adams monthly in Cincinnati charged that Jackson's wife, Rachel, was a bigamist. When Rachel suddenly died at 61 only weeks after the election, Jackson blamed the magazine's slander for her death, and never forgave Adams for not putting a stop to it.

"To the Polls! To the Polls!" commanded the *United States Telegraph* and other newspapers in 1828, and the voters responded. Four times as many men voted for president in 1828 as in 1824, and, together, Irish workmen, midwestern farmers, and southern planters gave Andrew Jackson a huge victory, with 56% of the popular vote. This is an ordinary landslide by modern standards, but in the 19th century the margin was enormous, unsurpassed until Theodore Roosevelt was reelected with 60% of the vote in 1904. Jackson not only swept the South and the Midwest, he also took the nation's two most populous states, New York and Pennsylvania. The electoral vote in 1828 was 178 for Jackson and only 83 for Adams. John Quincy Adams, like his father, would be a one-term president.

Historians still argue about whether Jackson's victory in 1828 signified the rise of the common man or merely the rise of the professional politician. The answer, of course, is both. Until the 1820s it was enough for leaders to appeal to only a few thousand men of property and education. Afterward, they had to reach millions of ordinary people, and to do this they formed political parties.

The noble old ideal of impartial, nonpartisan leadership, favored by the Founding Fathers and the first six presidents, ended with the election of Andrew Jackson. A new system began with two well-organized but constantly brawling political parties, and every four years the winner-take-all method of awarding electoral votes has kept the two-party system stable by making it difficult for third and fourth parties to compete in presidential elections.

Nearly 200 years have passed since the House of Representatives last decided a presidential election, but the truth is we have been lucky. A competitive three- or four-party race for president can happen again anytime, and when it does, there will be nothing to prevent the election from being decided by another one-state-one-vote farce.

CHAPTER 7

1968

A Close Call with George Wallace

THE 1968 PRESIDENTIAL ELECTION ALMOST WENT TO THE HOUSE OF Representatives. Alabama's segregationist governor, George Wallace, received 13.5% of the popular vote, took five southern states, and won 46 electoral votes. But late in September, only five weeks before Election Day, polls had given Wallace 22% of the vote. Even if this figure had fallen to 19%, Wallace would still have had enough support to win four more southern states, including Florida, and the electoral vote would have been Richard Nixon 256, Hubert Humphrey 191, and Wallace 91. Then, for the first time since 1824, no presidential candidate would have won a majority of the electoral vote, and Wallace, holding the balance of power, would have demanded a rollback of civil rights.

Instead, on the morning of October 3, Wallace lost 40% of his support in one disastrous seven-minute press conference.

───◆───

In the 1960s many people looked at the era's great social changes with fear. Most Americans supported the Civil Rights Act of 1964 and the Voting Rights Act of 1965, but they were wary of Supreme Court decisions that reversed criminal convictions when the police found evidence illegally, or when the police failed to tell a defendant about his or her right to remain silent or have a lawyer. Crime in America doubled during the 1960s, and while the Supreme Court's rulings had little to do with the rise, many people denounced the high court anyway as crime spread rapidly from inner-city slums to working-class neighborhoods nearby.

The number of people on welfare also doubled in the 1960s. By the end of the decade, nearly 500,000 Blacks (the term was replacing "Negroes") were on welfare in New York City alone. Although the cost of this growth in relief payments was only ⅓ of 1% of a taxpayer's income, blue-collar workers hated these "handouts" to Blacks and blamed welfare for the steep rise in taxes as federal, state, and local governments struggled to pay for the Vietnam War, wage increases, and new government services such as Medicare and Medicaid. Instead of taxing the few to help the many, which is how most voters saw Franklin Roosevelt's New Deal in the 1930s, Lyndon Johnson's Great Society often seemed to be taxing the many to help the few.

Even in the North, more and more voters began to see racial progress as a threat to their schools, unions, and neighborhoods, and integration as causing a decline in home values. But just as white enthusiasm for civil rights was cooling, Blacks were growing more militant. "We have been saying freedom for six years—and we ain't got nothin'," said Black activist Stokely Carmichael. "What we are gonna start saying now is 'Black Power.'"

In 1966, the year Carmichael made headlines, 43 riots flared across the country, a result of the deep tension between the Blacks who lived in ghettos and the mostly white policemen who patrolled them. The following year was even more violent. In 1967, 83 people died in 164 riots, including 43 dead in Detroit and 23 in Newark. The carnage was televised, and soon the image of Blacks that many whites had was no longer that of a peaceful preacher being beaten by a southern sheriff, but instead a young thug shouting "Black Power!" while throwing a rock or a Molotov cocktail.

One did not have to be a racist to feel that liberal programs weren't working. As Michigan congressman (and future president) Gerald Ford asked at the time:

> *How long are we going to abdicate law and order—the backbone of any civilization—in favor of a soft social theory that the man who*

heaves a brick through your window or tosses a fire-bomb into your car is simply the misunderstood and underprivileged product of a broken home?

Above all, it was court-ordered school busing that hardened the outlook of white working-class voters. Many whites had no objection to busing Black children to all-white schools, but strongly opposed the busing of white children to all-Black schools, and the failure of judges and officials to distinguish between these two kinds of busing made many people see the national government as an oppressor rather than a protector. In city after city, the busing of white schoolchildren into Black ghettos embittered not only their parents, but their entire extended families, and drove millions of white voters away from the Democratic Party for decades.

❦

The man who expressed the resentment that many whites felt in 1968 was Governor George Wallace of Alabama. Wallace rarely talked about Blacks or segregation directly. He spoke instead about "law and order," telling audiences, "It's a sad day in the country when you can't talk about law and order without someone calling you a racist."

"We don't have riots in Alabama," Wallace explained to a packed crowd at Madison Square Garden in October 1968. "First one of 'em to pick up a brick gets a bullet in the brain, that's all. And then you walk over to the next one and say, 'All right, pick up a brick. We just want to see you pick up one of them bricks now!'"

Wallace framed racial issues as a question of federal or local control. "The people don't like this triflin' with their children," he told columnist James Kilpatrick in 1967, "busing little boys and girls half across a city just to achieve 'the proper racial mix.' . . . Folks won't stand for it."

Wallace said that judges, professors, and government officials

have looked down their noses at the average man in the street too long. They look down at the bus driver, the truck driver, the beautician, the firemen, the policeman, and the steel worker, the plumber and the communications worker, and the oil worker and the little businessman, and they say, "We've gotta write a guideline. We've gotta tell you when to get up in the morning. We've gotta tell you when to go to bed at night."

Wallace told crowds, "When I'm president I'm goin' to gather all of these pointy-head bureaucrats . . . and sling their briefcases into the middle of the Potomac."

Audiences laughed, cheered, and gave Wallace money, and soon pollsters found that more than one out of five Americans wanted Wallace to be president.

George Corley Wallace was born in 1919 in Clio, Alabama, a village surrounded by cotton, corn, and peanut fields in the southeastern corner of the state. His father was a farmer who still plowed land with a mule, although in the early 1930s voters elected him chairman of Barbour County's Board of Revenue. Wallace's mother was a piano teacher.

As a boy, Wallace liked to fish and swim in Blue Springs, a lake where old Confederate veterans sometimes held reunions. He also boxed with his brothers in a home-built ring in his backyard, and at 17 won the bantamweight (113–118 lbs.) championship in Alabama's Golden Gloves Tournament, winning again the following year. Wallace liked fights to be fair, however, and once rescued a Black boy from three white bullies.

In high school, Wallace was president of his senior class. He also won a summer job as a page in the state legislature after writing letters to all 35 of Alabama's state senators. At the University of Alabama, Wallace earned the money to go to college and law school by washing dishes, waiting tables, laying steam pipes, and driving an asphalt truck. During his last year in law school, Wallace met his wife, Lurleen Burns, a pretty but shy 16-year-old who worked at a five-and-dime store in Tuscaloosa.

After Wallace graduated from law school in 1942, he enlisted in the US Army Air Force, then married Lurleen before he was sent to the Pacific. While receiving training as a flight mechanic on a B-29 bomber, Wallace sometimes toyed with northern enlisted men, pretending to be an illiterate hillbilly who couldn't even read the signs outside a bathroom.

But at other times he told his fellow soldiers, "I'm going to be governor of Alabama someday, you boys wait and see." The ambitious Wallace sent hundreds of Christmas cards every year to voters in Barbour County, some from flight-training schools in the Rocky Mountains, others from air force bases in the Pacific. Each one said, "Merry Christmas, your friend, George Wallace."

By 1945, Staff Sergeant Wallace was under the command of General Curtis LeMay, the gruff, cigar-smoking aviator who had perfected the art of firebombing Japanese cities with napalm. During the last month of World War II, on the night of July 19, Wallace's crew and 126 other B-29s each dropped 14,000 pounds of bombs on Fukui, an industrial city of 300,000 people on Japan's west coast, burning 85% of the town. The intense heat pushed Wallace's plane up thousands of feet and knocked out two of its four engines. The plane then fell 16,000 feet, but the pilot somehow managed to level the B-29 while dodging antiaircraft fire, and Wallace, working frantically at the instrument panel, restarted both engines.

On their way home, the entire crew, exhausted, fell asleep and veered 150 miles off course before someone finally woke up. With the plane dangerously short of fuel, Wallace adjusted the engines several times during the last leg of the trip, shifting fuel from one tank to another. When the B-29 finally landed, it ran out of gas on the way from the runway to the hangar; the plane had come that close to crashing.

Two weeks after the war ended, Wallace refused to take part in a routine training flight in California. "I've done my share," he said. "I'm not going to fly anymore." Puzzled, Wallace's superiors ordered him to a hospital, and doctors concluded that he was suffering anemia, anorexia, and severe anxiety. Within weeks, Wallace received an honorable discharge.

Home at last, Wallace was elected to Alabama's house of representatives in 1946, and circuit judge in 1952. He and Lurleen had four children, and in 1958, when he was still only 39, Wallace ran for governor.

Wallace spoke to voters about Alabama's need for more roads, better schools, and new industry, and criticized his chief opponent, John Patterson, for "rolling with the new wave of the [Ku Klux] Klan and its terrible tradition of lawlessness." But Patterson beat Wallace by 65,000 votes. Afterward, according to biographer Marshall Frady, Wallace told his aides, "John Patterson out-niggahed me. And boys, I'm not gonna to be out-niggahed again."

In 1962 Wallace ran for governor once more, attacking a "lousy federal court system" for trying to destroy "our very way of life." Radio ads urged listeners to "Vote right—Vote white—Vote for the Fighting Judge," and this time Wallace won. On Inauguration Day, January 14, 1963, Wallace became a national figure immediately when he said, "I draw a line in the dust . . . and I say, segregation now, segregation tomorrow, and segregation forever." The phrase was coined by his speechwriter, Asa Earl Carter, a right-wing radio host and Ku Klux Klansman who routinely denounced Blacks, Jews, and Yankees, and was once part of a group that castrated a Black handyman chosen at random.

"I started off talking about schools and highways and prisons and taxes—and I couldn't make them listen," Wallace told newspaper editor Louis Eckl. "Then I began talking about niggers—and they stomped the floor."

While Wallace was governor, the state built new roads, hospitals, and community colleges, and paid for them with a 4% sales tax that applied even to food. (Not surprisingly, the next time Wallace ran for office, he received many campaign contributions from building and road contractors.)

Wallace's most famous moment as governor came when he kept his promise to Alabama's voters to "stand in front of the schoolhouse door" to try to prevent Black students from enrolling at the University of Alabama. On June 11, 1963, behind a podium in front of the doors to Foster Auditorium, where students registered for their courses, Wallace declared that the people of Alabama "denounce and forbid this illegal and unwarranted action by the central government." But Assistant US Attorney General Nicholas Katzenbach, who worked for Robert Kennedy and had National Guard troops to back him up, was unmoved. "I'm not interested in this show," he said. "The students [sitting in nearby cars] will register today. They will go to school tomorrow."

Although Wallace's staged confrontation did not prevent the integration of the University of Alabama, his legal defeat was a political victory.

His popularity soared, not only among southerners, but with lower-income whites in the North too. When Wallace challenged President Lyndon Johnson in three Democratic primaries in 1964, he won 30% of the vote in Indiana, 34% of the vote in Wisconsin, and 43% of the vote in Maryland.

Still handsome in his late 40s, Wallace moved with youthful vigor. He stabbed the air with his finger to make a point, and often widened or rolled his dark brown eyes for comic effect. When he chose, he could also narrow his eyes and curl his lips to form a snarl. Five-feet-seven-and-a-half-inches, Wallace wore off-the-rack suits and ordinary ties, and smoked inexpensive White Owl cigars. He never drank, and rarely ate much. As a friend from his hometown said, "He ain't got but one serious appetite, and that's votes."

Because Alabama law at the time prohibited a governor from serving two consecutive terms, Wallace asked the state legislature to change the law in 1965. But only the house of representatives complied; Alabama's senate balked. Undeterred, Wallace had his wife, Lurleen, run for governor in 1966 even though she was recovering from cancer. Quiet, dull, and melancholy, Lurleen nevertheless received more votes in the Democratic Party's gubernatorial primary than her nine opponents combined, and every state senator who had voted against allowing Wallace run for a second term as governor was soundly defeated by a triumphant Wallace supporter.

Lurleen was governor for only a year and a half, however. She died May 7, 1968, after a new round of cancer. Wallace spent several weeks mourning, then resumed his new campaign for the presidency as a third-party candidate.

In 1967 Wallace raised over $500,000 to pay for the tedious work of collecting the more than one million signatures needed to put his American Independent Party on the ballot in all 50 states the following year. Explaining why the country needed a third party, Wallace compared Democrats Lyndon Johnson, Hubert Humphrey, and Robert Kennedy to Republicans Richard Nixon, Nelson Rockefeller, and Michigan governor George Romney (the father of Mitt Romney) and said, "There's not a dime's worth of difference in any of them!"

By the summer of 1968, Wallace was on the ballot in every state except Ohio, where Democrats and Republicans had together passed a tough law that required third-party candidates for president to collect more than 400,000 signatures to get on the state's ballot. Wallace sued, claiming that his right to due process had been violated, and, ironically, the same US Supreme Court that he had criticized so often ruled 6 to 3 in his favor and ordered Ohio to put Wallace on its ballot. Wallace's American Independent Party, now a 50-state force, was America's first right-wing third party of any size since Millard Fillmore led the Know-Nothings in 1856.

Wallace's goal was to prevent both the Republican and the Democratic presidential candidates from winning a majority of the electoral vote. "When this happens," Wallace said, "I would not be the next president of the United States. But I would have the power to say just who *would* be the next president. And I make no secret that I would want something in return before I make my choice." One thing he would insist on, Wallace told audiences, "there won't be one thin dime available from federal funds to pay for all this school busin'—you can rely on that."

Wallace asked for, and received, notarized affidavits from all 535 of his potential electors that pledged that, if elected, they would vote only for Wallace himself or anyone else that Wallace might endorse. (The number of affidavits was 535 and not 538 because Wallace did not run in the District of Columbia, where nearly 70% of the voters were Black.)

For all the anger he tapped into, Wallace could also make his audiences laugh. "The only four-letter words hippies don't know are w-o-r-k and s-o-a-p," he said, and when protestors called him a fascist, he said, "I was killing fascists when you punks were in diapers." Often Wallace blew a kiss to demonstrators, which to the delight of his supporters, only made the protesters angrier.

During the first few months of 1968, Wallace's support in the national polls was only about 10%. But after Martin Luther King was assassinated on April 4, and rioting continued for a week in more than 100 cities (including just two blocks from the White House) with 39 dead and almost 20,000 arrested, the national mood changed. Most whites did not want to hear any more about racial injustice. They were too appalled by Black violence and frightened by Black militants.

From April onward, the 1968 presidential campaign would be fought on Wallace's preferred ground: law and order. It displaced even the Vietnam War as the prime issue of the year, as Wallace began to appeal to meat-packers in Wisconsin, steelworkers in Indiana, and construction workers in New York. "We're gonna have a police state for folks who burn the cities down," Wallace told them. "They aren't gonna burn anymore cities."

Polls showed that 80% of Americans believed that law enforcement was breaking down, but the phrase "law and order" also spoke to a yearning for quieter, shorter-haired students, marriage before sex, and safer, all-white neighborhoods. Richard Nixon, the Republican presidential candidate, ran television ads showing a woman walking down a dark street as an announcer noted ominously, "Crimes of violence in the United States have almost doubled in recent years."

Wallace appealed to the nation's desire for order more crudely. When demonstrators in New York lay down in front of President Johnson's motorcade to protest the Vietnam War, Wallace won roars of approval when he told audiences "any anarchists lie down in front of my automobile, it'll be the very last time they lie down in front of anything."

The nation's hunger for order grew even stronger after the Democratic Party's violent convention in August. Enraged by the chants of 15,000 antiwar protesters who were ridiculing the Democratic presidential candidate, Hubert Humphrey (who the protestors called "the Gutless Wonder"), an equal number of Chicago police officers and Illinois National Guardsmen charged toward the demonstrators, shouting "Kill! Kill!" as they clubbed anyone who moved near the convention arena, even news reporters covering the event. Those who were not being beaten chanted, "The whole world is watching!"—and it was true. Television coverage shifted from the convention indoors to the violence outdoors, and left millions of Americans feeling that the Democrats could not keep order and that Democratic policies had led to lawlessness.

One result of the convention, little noticed at the time, was a vote by the delegates, 1,350 to 1,206, to adopt new rules to end the predominance

of boss-picked delegates and increase the number of primaries and cau-
cuses in future presidential elections.

In the weeks that followed the disastrous convention, Humphrey's
campaign nearly collapsed. Humphrey had little money, and in September polls showed that his national support had fallen to 29%, less than half
of Johnson's support in 1964. Crowds at Humphrey's rallies shouted "End
the War!" and "Dump the Hump!" In Seattle, antiwar protestors condemned Humphrey's "crimes against humanity," then stormed the stage,
saying, "We've come to arrest you." "Knock it off!" Humphrey shouted
before policemen cleared the overcrowded stage.

In the South, only about 10% of the whites supported Humphrey.
Even in the North, a secret AFL-CIO survey of its members showed that
one-third of the country's union laborers favored Wallace.

In a televised speech on September 30, Humphrey finally broke with
President Johnson and said, "As president, I would be willing to stop the
bombing of North Vietnam as an acceptable risk for peace because it
could lead to success in the negotiations." But the speech was late. With
only five weeks left before Election Day, the time for a Humphrey come-
back was running out.

By contrast, Wallace's support in the polls climbed to 16% after the
riots following Martin Luther King's assassination, and to 22% (only 7%
behind Humphrey) after the violence in Chicago. Wallace was ahead in
nine southern states, so if Humphrey could narrow Nixon's lead even
slightly, an electoral deadlock was possible.

Across the country, hundreds of thousands of Wallace supporters
mailed small checks to Post Office Box 1968 in Montgomery, Alabama,
although Wallace and his campaign workers continued to fly on a DC-6
propeller plane rather than a Boeing jet. Fried chicken tycoon Colonel
Harlan Sanders sent Wallace a six-figure donation, and John Wayne
mailed Wallace three checks of $10,000 each, writing on one, "Sock it to
'em, George!" One question that worried polling firms was whether Wallace's support might be even higher than 22% if some voters, especially in
the North, were reluctant to tell a pollster that they favored the Alabama
governor.

Thomas Sutton, a New York City construction worker, explained why he gave money to Wallace:

> *I'm not against the Negro; he's got to have a fair crack the same as anyone else. And some of the best fellows I work with—best at hard work, I mean—are Negroes . . . But in my opinion there's a hell of a lot more who don't want to work, who are happy to live off welfare, and it's my money going to support them. . . .*
>
> *All these liberal intellectuals, they don't understand us. What contact do they have with us? We fix their cars or paint their houses or sweep their drives, but they never see us.*
>
> *They've got this great guilt thing about the Negro and integration and all, so we have to be forced to do things: our children have to be bused to different schools; we have to sell our houses to Negroes. They don't because there isn't a Negro in a thousand with the money to buy their kind of houses, and anyway they send kids to private schools.*
>
> *Well I'd just like to redress the balance. One law for the Negro and the white working man and the rich liberals. I think Wallace will do that. I think he'll be fair to all. And I think he'll be tough with young hoodlums.* *

Even with 22% of Americans supporting him, Wallace could not run for president without a vice presidential running mate, and no one in Congress was willing to break with his party to run with him. Wallace sent an inquiry to FBI Director J. Edgar Hoover, but Hoover did not even bother to reply. Ezra Taft Benson, who had been President Eisenhower's secretary of agriculture, did express some interest in running with Wallace, but he was a Mormon, and the leaders of the Mormon Church, fearing bad publicity if they were associated with Wallace, barred him from running.

In August Wallace was considering Kentucky's Albert "Happy" Chandler, who between 1935 and 1960 had served two terms as the state's governor, one term as a US senator, and six years as the commissioner of

---

* David English, *Divided They Stand* (Englewood Cliffs, NJ: Prentice-Hall, 1969), 355.

Major League Baseball. Chandler could have increased Wallace's support in the Border South, and at 70, he was interested in running because he was bored playing golf.

But Wallace's supporters in Kentucky, along with several Texan oil barons who had given money to Wallace, and even some of Wallace's own aides, balked at nominating a moderate. As governor, Chandler had once sent the Kentucky National Guard to a town that was resisting integration. "It's not my job to put Blacks in the school," he said at the time, "but if they show up, it's my job to see they are protected." Chandler had also desegregated Kentucky's parks, and it was when he was baseball's commissioner that Jackie Robinson began playing for the Brooklyn Dodgers.

By September, Wallace still did not have a running mate. Earlier in the summer he had asked Curtis LeMay, the retired four-star general who had modernized the Strategic Air Command, to run with him. Wallace wanted to attract some of the many college-educated conservatives who had voted for Barry Goldwater in 1964. But LeMay declined to run with Wallace because he did not like his views on segregation. In the early 1950s LeMay had fully integrated the Strategic Air Command without any problems or delay.

As Election Day grew closer, however, LeMay was alarmed when both Humphrey and Nixon talked about winding down the Vietnam War with troop withdrawals and peace negotiations. To LeMay, Wallace was the only presidential candidate willing to trust the Vietnam War to the generals, the professionals who knew how to win a war.

On September 27 in Chicago, Wallace met with LeMay a second time and assured him that he was not a racist, and that he opposed letting the Soviet Union have as many nuclear missiles as the United States. Wallace told LeMay that his vice presidential candidacy would be an opportunity to educate Americans on defense matters, and that Texas oilman Bunker Hunt would pay LeMay $1 million to reimburse him for the loss of his job as chairman of Network Electronics, a California firm that had no desire to be associated with the Wallace campaign.

LeMay agreed to run. Had LeMay declined again, Wallace was planning to run with Jimmie Davis, the rabid segregationist and former governor of Louisiana who was best known for writing the song "You Are My Sunshine."

✦

Curtis Emerson LeMay, whose career progressed from biplanes to supersonic jets, was born in 1906 in Columbus, Ohio, the son of a steelworker. As a boy, he delivered newspapers to earn money to buy a rifle and a radio. At Ohio State, LeMay was an ROTC student majoring in civil engineering until his family's lack of money forced him to leave college and join the Ohio National Guard instead. LeMay trained to be a pilot, and joined the Army Air Corps in 1930. He mastered instrument flying and navigation, but switched from fighter planes to bombers when he realized that dogfights would not win wars.

By 1943 LeMay, at 37, was the youngest lieutenant general in the army. He had developed the precision daylight attack, targeting individual German factories while Britain's Royal Air Force, with much less accuracy, bombed cities at night. LeMay's men called him "Old Ironpants" because the general insisted that his pilots fly right through antiaircraft fire without taking evasive action, which always reduced a bomber's accuracy. Leading by example, LeMay headed several of these missions himself.

In January 1945 LeMay took over the 21st Bomber Command on the Marianas Islands, within flying distance of Japan. Previous bombing raids over Tokyo had done little damage because once the B-29s reached their cruising altitude of 30,000 feet, the jet stream buffeted the planes and made bombing accuracy impossible. LeMay decided that his B-29s should fly at 5,000 to 9,000 feet instead, because at an altitude this low, Japanese antiaircraft gunners would not have enough time to fire a useful barrage at the planes. LeMay also concluded that because most of Japan's buildings were made of wood, firebombing its cities with napalm and other flammable chemicals would inflict the most damage.

The attacks were devastating. On March 9, 1945, 346 bombers burned one-sixth of Tokyo and killed 83,000 people, with a loss of only 14 planes. Two nights later, bombers destroyed Nagoya, Japan's third-largest city, and two nights after that, they bombed Osaka, Japan's second-largest city. After this, about half of Japan's city-dwellers fled for the countryside.

One statistician assigned to the 21st Bomber Command was Captain Robert McNamara, the future secretary of defense. He heard a pilot ask General LeMay why his plane had to fly as low as 5,000 feet, where his men were vulnerable to antiaircraft fire. "Losses hurt me as much as you," LeMay said. "But you lost one wingman and we destroyed Tokyo." McNamara later joked that it was the longest speech he ever heard the un-talkative general give.

Blunt, humorless, and usually chomping a cigar, the heavy-set LeMay often had a scowl. Years later, it was LeMay who movie director Stanley Kubrick had in mind when he filmed *Dr. Strangelove*, with its memorable character, Air Force General Buck Turgidson, played by George C. Scott.

In 1948, when LeMay took over the Strategic Air Command, not one bomber group was combat ready. Soon SAC was on a wartime footing 24 hours a day. B-36 (and later B-52) bombers were ready to fly from one continent to another, each with a detailed flight plan and the ability to be refueled in the middle of a flight. LeMay was also in charge of the Berlin Airlift that flew food and supplies to West Berlin after the Soviets had cut off all of the roads and railways to the city.

During the Cuban Missile Crisis in 1962, LeMay advocated carpet bombing all nine of the Soviet Union's missile sites in Cuba. As the US Air Force's chief of staff, LeMay planned an attack that included the use of 90 tactical nuclear weapons. Fortunately, a naval blockade was sufficient to persuade the Soviets to remove their nuclear missiles, but LeMay bitterly resented President Kennedy's reluctance to use force, which he saw as weakness. LeMay's dislike of Kennedy turned to hostility after the United States signed the Nuclear Test Ban Treaty in 1963, which the general strongly opposed.

In 1965 LeMay, at 58, retired from the military and published a memoir, *Mission with LeMay*, that was coauthored by a friend, MacKinlay Kantor. At the end of the book, the authors said that the United States should tell the North Vietnamese to "stop their aggression or we're going to bomb them back into the Stone Age." Although the book was primarily written by Kantor and only lightly proofread by LeMay, LeMay never backed away from the "Stone Age" sentence, and it remains the quote for which he is most famous (or infamous).

Three years later, LeMay wrote another book, *America Is in Danger*, which said that nuclear deterrence must rely "not upon the ability to with-stand a first strike and retaliate effectively, but on the ability to launch a first strike and win if necessary."

~ ~

On October 3, 1968, at the Hilton Hotel in Pittsburgh, George Wallace introduced Curtis LeMay as his vice presidential running mate at a press conference that was broadcast live by all three major television networks. Only a few minutes before, three of Wallace's aides had urged General LeMay not to talk about nuclear weapons. They were right to be worried.

After Wallace's announcement, the first question for LeMay came from a reporter for the *Los Angeles Times*: "General, do you think it is necessary to use nuclear weapons to win the war in Vietnam?"

"No," LeMay said, "we can win this war without nuclear weapons." And if LeMay had stopped there, the outcome of 1968's election might have been quite different. But he continued:

> But I have to say that we seem to have a phobia about using nuclear weapons . . . I think there may be times when it would be most efficient to use nuclear weapons. However, the public opinion in this country and throughout the world throw up their hands in horror . . .

LeMay added that he would rather "be killed by a nuclear bomb than a rusty knife."

"I don't believe the world would end if we exploded a nuclear weapon," LeMay persisted.

> I've seen a film of Bikini Atoll after twenty tests, and the fish are all back in the lagoons, the coconut trees are growing coconuts, the guava bushes have fruit on them, the birds are back. As a matter of fact, everything is about the same except the land crabs . . . the land crabs

are a little bit hot, and there's a question about whether you should eat a land crab or not.*

At this point Wallace rushed to the microphones and said, "Now let me say, General LeMay hasn't advocated the use of nuclear weapons, not at all. He discussed nuclear weapons with you. He's against the use of nuclear weapons, and I am too."

LeMay tried to help too, but only made things worse. "I'll be damned lucky," he said, "if I don't appear as a drooling idiot whose only solution to any problem is to drop atomic bombs all over the world. I assure you, I'm not."

The press conference lasted only seven minutes, but the damage was done. Wallace lost 40% of his support in the next few days, and the decline was even steeper among northern women. Wallace quickly sent LeMay on a "fact-finding" tour of Vietnam so that the general could be as far from the campaign as possible. Wallace also faced hecklers with new signs that said "Bombs Away with Curt LeMay" and "Vote for Wallace—and the End of the World."

Meanwhile, the labor unions worked hard for Hubert Humphrey. In contrast to their rank and file, few labor leaders were for Wallace, and in October they campaigned day and night for the vice president. The AFL-CIO mailed 55 million leaflets to its members, and local unions mailed another 60 million. They reminded workers that Alabama was a low-wage state where unions were hard to form; that it had a high sales tax, even on food; and that the state was trying to convince companies to close union-manned factories in the North and open non-union plants in the South. The unions also pointed out that Alabama had almost no minimum wage laws or child labor statutes beyond what was federally required, and that in spite of Wallace's cry for "law and order," the state had the highest murder rate in the country.

The union efforts paid off. By the middle of October, Humphrey had cut Nixon's lead in half, to just 8%, and pulled 20 points ahead of

---

* Dan T. Carter, *The Politics of Rage* (New York: Simon & Schuster, 1995), 359; Lewis Chester, Godfrey Hodgson, and Bruce Page, *An American Melodrama: The Presidential Campaign of 1968* (New York: Viking, 1969), 699; and David English, *Divided They Stand*, op. cit., 359.

Wallace. Humphrey's speech calling for a bombing halt in North Vietnam also helped. "If You Mean It, We're With You," said one student's sign. To Humphrey's relief, there were no more hecklers for the rest of his campaign.

In Texas, President Johnson, who supported Humphrey, summoned the state's two feuding leaders: John Connally, the state's conservative governor, and Ralph Yarborough, its liberal senator. "We're not going to see Texas go to the Republicans," the president told them. "Hubert needs help. Now get the lead out of your pants and give him the help he needs." They did, and Texas was the only southern state besides Kentucky where Humphrey won twice as many votes as Wallace.

By November, both the Gallup and Harris polls showed Humphrey only 2% behind Nixon. "It's the women," said pollster Lou Harris, "the women are for peace."

━━◆━━

Whether his lead was large or small, Richard Nixon had led in every poll throughout the year. He charged Humphrey with doing nothing while "50% of American women are frightened to walk within a mile of their homes at night." Nixon's vice presidential running mate, Governor Spiro Agnew of Maryland, also stressed the need for law and order, especially when he campaigned in the Border South, where Wallace was threatening Nixon's lead.

In South Carolina, Nixon successfully persuaded Senator Strom Thurmond to join the Republican Party by promising to oppose busing and appoint conservative justices to the Supreme Court. South Carolina was the only state in the Deep South that Wallace didn't win; the vote there was Nixon 38%, Wallace 32%, and Humphrey 30%.

Nixon was careful to support civil rights in general even while promising only a minimal enforcement of court-ordered busing and school desegregation. When someone asked Nixon to campaign in a Black area of Philadelphia, he refused, saying, "I am not going to campaign for the Black vote at the risk of alienating the suburban vote."

Nixon knew that Wallace was taking twice as many votes away from him as he was from Humphrey, and that even after LeMay's terrible press conference, Wallace continued to draw tens of thousands of people to rallies in northern cities such as Boston, New York, and Detroit. But as more polls showed Humphrey catching up to Nixon, many Wallace supporters began to worry that a vote for Wallace could allow Humphrey to edge past Nixon and win the election.

"Do you want to get something off your chest or do you want to get something done?" Nixon asked Wallace supporters. "Do you want a moment's satisfaction from your vote of protest, or do you want four years of action?"

———

On Election Day, November 5, 1968, 73 million Americans went to the polls. The election was one of the closest in American history, and many people wondered whether Wallace might succeed in preventing both Nixon and Humphrey from winning a majority of the electoral vote. Not until the following morning, when Illinois and Missouri finally went for Nixon, was it clear that the election would not go to the House of Representatives.

Richard Nixon won 43.4% of the popular vote, Hubert Humphrey was close with 42.7%, and George Wallace won 13.5%. More important, Nixon won the presidency with 301 electoral votes. (He should have won 302 electoral votes, but he lost a vote in December when a North Carolina elector pledged to Nixon voted for Wallace instead.) Humphrey took 191 electoral votes, and Wallace, by winning five states (Georgia, Alabama, Mississippi, Louisiana, and Arkansas, plus the one additional vote in North Carolina), received 46 electoral votes. Of all the third-party candidates in American history, only Theodore Roosevelt has won more electoral votes than Wallace.

In the South, the Democratic Party collapsed. The 1968 election was the first where the Democrats lost both the Deep South and the Border South simultaneously, as white southerners, who had given Franklin Roosevelt more than 80% of their votes in the 1930s, gave Humphrey less than 15% of their votes this time. Humphrey's support among southern whites was probably below 10% if you subtract Mexican Americans,

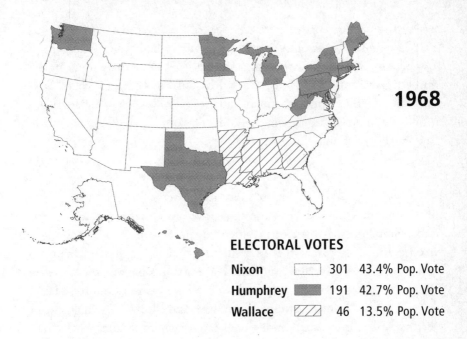

1968

ELECTORAL VOTES

Nixon	☐	301	43.4% Pop. Vote
Humphrey	▓	191	42.7% Pop. Vote
Wallace	▨	46	13.5% Pop. Vote

Cuban Americans, Jews in Atlanta and Florida, and members of the United Mine Workers.

After 1968, the South's influence within the Democratic Party declined quickly as more and more southern voters and politicians abandoned their traditional party to become Republicans instead. The South would become solidly Republican for the next half century, and as a consequence, the character of the Republican Party has grown increasingly southern. One of Wallace's lasting legacies is that he moved the Republican Party further to the right.

In the North, the Democratic totals were also grim. Humphrey outpolled the combined vote of Nixon and Wallace in only six states—Massachusetts, Rhode Island, Maine, Hawaii, Minnesota, and New York—but even in New York, Humphrey outpolled the other two candidates by only ⅕ of 1% of the vote.

Wallace may have been too coarse and too much of a Deep South racist to be elected president, but 41% of his 10 million votes came from the North and the West, where on average he received 8% of the vote. Wallace won the votes of 22% of the nation's Italian Americans, almost 16% of America's union workers, and nearly 20% of the people in the southern halves of Ohio, Indiana, and Missouri. By contrast, when "Dixiecrat" Strom Thurmond ran for president in 1948, he was on the ballot in only two non-southern states, California and North Dakota, and in California he won only ⅟₃₀ of 1% of the vote.

—

If Wallace had ignored his more racist supporters and had chosen Kentucky's Happy Chandler, a former governor and senator and an experienced campaigner, as his vice presidential running mate, Wallace might have held on to most of the 22% support that he enjoyed in September before General LeMay frightened so many people away. With even 19% of the vote nationwide, Wallace would have won four more states—North Carolina, South Carolina, Tennessee, and Florida—giving him 91 electoral votes, more than enough to deny Richard Nixon an electoral majority.

Even if Wallace's share of the popular vote had dropped to 17% (rather than his final total of 13.5%), this would still have been enough for him to take the Carolinas and Tennessee and win 77 electoral votes. Then, if Happy Chandler had campaigned well in Missouri, a state that borders his home state of Kentucky, and taken only 2% more of the votes away from Nixon there, Missouri might have gone for Humphrey rather than Nixon, and the electoral vote would have been a deadlock: Nixon 259, Humphrey 202, and Wallace 77.

How would a deadlock have unfolded? Wallace almost certainly would have tried to use the six weeks between Election Day and the Monday in mid-December when the electors actually vote for president to try to make a deal with Nixon. He would have asked Nixon to promise to appoint only conservative judges to the Supreme Court, a request that by itself Nixon might have agreed to. But probably Wallace would also have asked Nixon to promise to stop enforcing court-ordered busing, open housing laws, and labor regulations that were requiring unions to change their rules if they favored whites with seniority over Blacks who had none. Wallace would also have asked for deep cuts in foreign aid.

A limited concession by Nixon to Wallace might have been possible, but a wide-ranging deal with Wallace would have been radioactive, morally discrediting Nixon as president even before he was inaugurated.

In the absence of a deal with Nixon, Wallace's choices would have been difficult. He might have accepted a vague pledge from Nixon, declared victory, and run for president again in 1972 if Nixon's promise seemed unfulfilled. Or seeking a better deal, Wallace might have held on to his electoral votes, denied Nixon an electoral majority, and taken his chances in the House of Representatives.

If the 1968 election had shifted to the House, it is hard to know what would have happened. The balloting would have been held on a one-state-one-vote basis, with 26 states required for a candidate to win. In January 1969, 19 states had Republican majorities in their congressional delegations, and 5 more states had delegations that were evenly divided between the Republicans and the Democrats, and therefore would have been unable to vote. The other 26 states had Democratic majorities, but 12 of these states were southern, and it is highly unlikely that all 12 of the southern Democratic congressional delegations would have voted for Humphrey. If even one of these 12 southern delegations had declined to vote for Humphrey, no one would have had a 26-state majority.

The Senate had a 57–43 Democratic majority in 1969, but under the Constitution the Senate is limited to voting only between the top two vice presidential candidates—i.e., for Nixon's running mate, Governor Spiro Agnew of Maryland, or for Humphrey's running mate, Senator Edmund Muskie of Maine. It is probable the Senate's Democrats would have chosen Muskie as vice president, as he was a respected and well-liked member of the Senate.

In the middle of such a mess, many of the southern Democrats in Congress, especially those from the states that Wallace won, might have tried to make their own deal with Nixon. Such a pact would have been more acceptable to the public than a direct deal between Nixon and Wallace, so it is likely that Nixon would have been willing to negotiate with them, although the horse-trading might have taken some time. If Nixon had not yet put together a 26-state majority by January 20, the newly chosen vice president, Edmund Muskie, would have been sworn in as acting president until the House of Representatives finally formed a 26-state majority for Nixon.

─── ◆ ───

Because a nightmare like this was only narrowly avoided in 1968–69, it is not surprising that a Gallup poll at the time showed that 79% of the public opposed America's antiquated system of electoral votes. In fact, in 1969 the House of Representatives, by an overwhelming margin, 339 to 70, voted for a constitutional amendment authorizing the direct election of presidents by the voters, without any electors as intermediaries. In the Senate, however, a coalition of southern and small-state senators, fearing domination by the big northern states, blocked the proposed amendment from even coming to a vote, and the 54 senators who did favor direct elections did not have enough votes to break their filibuster.

The 46 senators who said "no" to direct elections, the most logical reform of our antiquated system, did the nation a disservice. A demagogue had nearly thrown the 1968 election to the House of Representatives, and most people knew it. The next time a third-party candidate with a strong regional base runs for president, we may not be so lucky.

CHAPTER 8

Direct Elections and Other Flawed Proposals to Fix Our System

DESPITE THEIR MERITS, THE TRADITIONAL ALTERNATIVES TO OUR electoral system should be viewed with skepticism. If they have not won the support of the two-thirds of Congress and the three-fourths of the state legislatures needed for a constitutional amendment by now, after more than a century of discussion, they probably never will. Still, they deserve a look.

DIRECT ELECTIONS

Talk to ordinary people about electoral votes, and the first question they ask is, "Why don't we just have regular elections?" Decade after decade, one poll after another has shown that two-thirds of the American people favor the direct election of the president with no electoral votes. Sixty-five percent of Americans supported direct elections in a Gallup poll in 1944, 67% favored them in another Gallup poll in 1980, and 72% of the people (including 60% of Republicans) supported direct elections in 2007, according to a poll by the *Washington Post*. Most of the nation's political science professors also favor direct elections, as does the League of Women Voters and about half of Congress.

The proposal is simple. After a nationwide count of the popular vote, the candidate with the most votes becomes president. That's it. Done.

For two centuries, direct elections have worked well in races for governor, senator, congressman, and mayor. They are fundamentally fair. Every vote in a direct election has the exact same weight, whether it is urban or rural, from a big state or a small state, from a swing state or a safe state.

Unfortunately, direct elections were rejected by conservative senators in 1969 and liberal senators in 1979. Both groups cited the Founding Fathers, who rejected direct elections in 1787 by 10 states to 1, with only Pennsylvania voting for them. The Framers were wary of direct elections for three reasons. Two are completely antiquated. One is not.

First, in an age when news still traveled by horseback, the Founders were afraid that ordinary people would not know enough about candidates from other states who lived hundreds of miles and weeks of riding away. Letting ordinary people vote for president, said Virginia's George Mason, would be like referring "a trial of colors to a blind man." With indirect elections, by contrast, there could be an "electoral college"* of well-educated men who were informed enough to vote for candidates from other states.

The second reason the Founders rejected direct elections is that southerners opposed them. Fewer southerners than northerners would be participating in a national election, and the southerners did not want to be outvoted. This is why they insisted that their slaves (or to be precise, three-fifths of them) be included in the apportionment of electoral votes and seats in the House of Representatives, even though the slaves themselves could not vote. From the South's point of view, electoral votes solved the problem of underpopulation. In the 1790s, for example, Pennsylvania had about the same number of free men and women as Virginia, but Pennsylvania had only 15 electoral votes, while Virginia had 21.

During the Constitutional Convention, Gouverneur Morris denounced the "three-fifths compromise" that gave the South extra congressmen and electoral votes:

---

* Many people who defend our system of electoral votes would still like to abolish the "college" of 538 men and women who meet six weeks after a presidential election. Just count the electoral votes on election night, they say, without any electors as intermediaries. But if there were no people serving as electors, then any election where no candidate received a majority of the electoral vote would automatically shift to the House of Representatives, where the balloting would be one-state-one-vote. Unfortunately, as long as electoral deadlocks are still resolved in this antiquated way, it is probably better to keep the "college" of 538 electors who meet in the 50 state capitals, because at least they would represent the 50 states more equitably than the House of Representatives could, given its strange one-state-one-vote procedure.

Upon what principle is it that slaves shall be computed in the representation? Are they men? Then make them citizens and let them vote. Are they property? Why then is no other property included?. . . The admission of slaves into the [Southern states'] representation, when fairly explained, comes to this:

that the inhabitant of Georgia and South Carolina who goes to the coast of Africa and, in defiance of the most sacred laws of humanity, tears away his fellow creatures from their dearest connections and damns them to the most cruel bondages, shall have more votes in a government instituted for the protection of the rights of mankind than the citizen of Pennsylvania and New Jersey who views with a laudable horror so nefarious a practice.

Although slavery has been illegal for 150 years, a variation of our electoral system's unfairness still exists. In 2012, 48% more people voted in Iowa than Arkansas, yet each state had the same number of electoral votes, six. Similarly, 28% more people voted in Oregon than in Oklahoma in 2012, but each state had seven electoral votes. By contrast, if we had a direct election for president, voter turnout would be rewarded, because all votes would be treated equally no matter where they were cast.

In fact, having electoral votes rather than direct elections may have delayed women's suffrage by several decades, because in a direct presidential election, any state that gave women the vote would instantly have doubled its national influence. Instead, because the number of electoral votes that a state possessed had no relation to the state's turnout, a state had no incentive to give women the vote beyond the virtue of the act itself.

Because southern states with a low voter turnout could lose a small bit of influence in a direct election, southern legislators may be less likely than northern legislators to vote for such a change. (New York and Florida, however, which both currently have 29 electoral votes, are an exception to the north-south pattern of voter turnout. In 2012 Florida, because it is a swing state with a high proportion of older voters, enjoyed a voter turnout 29% higher than that of New York, a "spectator" state with a younger population.)

The Founders' final argument against direct elections is as relevant today as it was in the 18th century: the fear that candidates would ignore the small states and concentrate instead on winning votes in the big cities. South Carolina's Charles Pinckney warned the Constitutional Convention that direct elections would enable the most populous states, by combining their votes, to dominate the small states, although Benjamin Franklin pointed out that Massachusetts, Pennsylvania, and Virginia had no interest in common to propel them to do this.

Gunning Bedford Jr., a delegate from Delaware who had been James Madison's roommate at Princeton, was unmoved by Franklin's remarks. He cautioned his colleagues that even a suggestion that the small states should lose their equality with the big states would cause Delaware's delegates to walk out of the convention and seek a military alliance with a European state instead. "There are foreign powers who will take us by the hand," Bedford warned, as George Washington glared at him with stern disapproval.

Two centuries later, in the 1970s, one of the main reasons that Utah's Senator Orrin Hatch, along with senators from Wyoming, Nevada, Mississippi, and South Carolina, opposed direct elections was a fear that people "outside of American urban areas would not see future presidential candidates." They were afraid that candidates in direct elections would run airport-to-airport "tarmac campaigns," flying from one big city to another and ignoring the rural areas in between.

Yet even under the present system, rural voters rarely see a presidential candidate. Unless a small state is a closely contested "swing state," it rarely gets a campaign visit. Currently, of the 13 states with four electoral votes or fewer, only New Hampshire is a swing state. As a result, none of the other 12 states ever receives more than a single quick visit from a presidential candidate during a campaign, and most of the smallest states do not even get this. Contrary to widespread belief, *small states are almost completely ignored in winner-take-all presidential campaigns, and therefore have a great deal to gain from electoral reform.*

Another objection to direct elections that the Founders never considered is that close elections might require a national recount. With electoral votes, a recount is only needed in one or two closely contested states. In 2000, for example, when Al Gore's national lead over George W. Bush averaged fewer than eight votes per precinct, it was hard enough to recount the votes of just four Florida counties. A national recount, with absentee ballots dribbling into 3,000 different counties, could be a chaotic, lawsuit-filled nightmare. (Clearly, a new federal election code creating a *nonpartisan* election agency to modernize voting methods and standardize recounts would be extremely helpful.)

The biggest problem with direct elections, however, is the issue of whether or not to have a runoff. Powerful arguments exist on both sides of the question. Without a runoff, an extremist can take power with as little as 37% of the vote, as Adolf Hitler did in Germany in 1932–33. This is why most proposals for direct elections require a runoff if no candidate has won 40% (or often 50%) of the vote.* A runoff gives the opponents of a dangerous candidate an opportunity to unite against him.

Unfortunately, once there is a runoff when a candidate fails to win 40% (or 50%) of the vote, the mere existence of the runoff creates a dangerous "second chance psychology," a comfort zone that tempts a voter to cast a preliminary protest vote for a radical candidate in the first round of an election, knowing that he or she can cast a safer vote in the runoff. This is especially true if a candidate needs 50% of the vote to avoid a runoff, because with a threshold this high, runoffs are much more likely.

With runoffs in place, the Republican and Democratic Parties could split apart if candidates who lose nomination fights bolt and form new parties rather than stay put and loyally support the nominees who defeated them. The lure of winning protest votes in the first round of balloting could also spur the creation of new single-issue parties, each one hoping to win the balance of power in a close election and exercise leverage all out of proportion to the party's actual support. Worse, if the new

---

* In Chile, when a Marxist candidate, Salvador Allende, won the presidential election in 1970 with only 36% of the vote in a three-way race, there was no provision for a runoff. Because Allende frightened the other 64% of Chile's voters (as well as America's CIA), General Augusto Pinochet felt that he had sufficient public support to overthrow Chile's troubled democracy and impose 16 years of brutal military rule.

fringe parties siphoned enough votes away from the older, more moderate parties, radical candidates could finish first and second in the opening round of an election with just 25% to 35% of the vote. Then, in the runoff, moderate voters would be forced to choose between two candidates who are extreme, corrupt, or unbalanced.

Louisiana endured such a runoff in 1991 when voters in the race for governor were forced to choose between Edwin Edwards, a likable but dishonest former governor who soon went to prison for corruption, and David Duke, a former Nazi backed by the Ku Klux Klan.

Even if a nightmarish runoff between extreme candidates never occurs, direct elections that require only 40% of the vote to avoid a runoff would probably entice some parties to try to win elections with just 41% or 42% of the vote, as Britain's Conservative and Labour Parties have often done. Preaching to a reliable base could become more important than winning the support of moderates. In a polarized election, a candidate despised by 59% of the people could easily become president.

Some people claim that the two-party system would continue to thrive under direct elections. In US races for governor since 1948, for example—all of which were direct elections—the winning candidate received 45% or more of the vote 98% of the time. In other words, very few third-party candidates have been elected governor. But even in the largest states, governors look to their party's presidential candidates for leadership, and if the national parties split apart, the state parties would too.

The more relevant examples of how direct elections would change politics are in Europe, where multiparty systems are common. Candidates in Europe routinely win office with just 35% of the vote, and xenophobic anti-immigrant parties thriving there include France's National Front, Italy's Northern League, Germany's National Democrats, the Netherlands' Freedom Party, Greece's Golden Dawn, Austria's Freedom Party, the Swiss People's Party, the Danish People's Party, Hungary's Jobbik, and the Finns Party.

One of the virtues of America's electoral system is that it requires candidates to win votes in many states, which forces a candidate to be moderate so that he or she can appeal to a wider portion of the electorate. American candidates have won the presidency with 47.5% or more of the vote in 34 of the last 38 elections,* a happy outcome that happens much less often in European democracies. Professor Judith Best at the State University of New York at Cortland, one of the leading and most persuasive defenders of America's electoral system, opposes direct elections and asks, "Why is it more democratic to have a 40% president [who finished first in a multiparty election] than to have a 47.8% percent president who was a runner-up by a mere whisker?" It is a legitimate question, although one powerful answer is "because he (or she) won the most votes."

Personally, I favor direct elections, with a runoff if no one wins 50% of the vote. But because of the valid fear that direct elections would inevitably lead to smaller and more strident political parties, the support for direct elections may never be great enough to win the two-thirds of the Congress and three-fourths of the state legislatures needed for a constitutional amendment. Direct elections may be the most obvious alternative to the electoral system, and for decade after decade, two-thirds of the public has consistently supported this reform. Yet for two centuries the direct election of a president has simply been too big a change to be enacted.

We need a "Plan B." This book offers one, but first, let's consider some other flawed alternatives.

THE BONUS PLAN
A variation of direct elections is the Bonus Plan, which gives the winner of the popular vote a "bonus" of 100 electoral votes. Proposed by historian Arthur Schlesinger Jr. and several professors of political science, this is really just the abolition of the electoral college in disguise. The flaws of the Bonus Plan are similar to the flaws with direct elections, including the likelihood that a party would try to win the presidency with only 40% or 41% of the vote.

---

* The four exceptions are Bill Clinton, who won the presidency with 43% of the vote in the three-party election of 1992; Richard Nixon, who won with 43% of the popular vote in the three-party election of 1968; Woodrow Wilson, who won with 42% of the vote in the four-party election of 1912; and Grover Cleveland, who won with 46% of the vote in the three-party election of 1892.

THE DISTRICT PLAN

Another commonly proposed alternative to the winner-take-all system is the District Plan. Although championed by Thomas Jefferson, John Quincy Adams, Martin Van Buren, and George H. W. Bush (who in 1969 also advocated direct elections), the District Plan has never won much support except in Maine, which adopted the plan in 1969, and Nebraska, which adopted it in 1992. In the District Plan, every congressional district has one electoral vote, and the other two electoral votes that each state has go to the state's popular-vote winner, just as they do under winner-take-all.

In 2008, for example, John McCain took two of Nebraska's three congressional districts, and also won the most votes statewide, so he won four of Nebraska's five electoral votes. But Barack Obama took the congressional district that includes Omaha, so he won one of the state's five electoral votes. (Nebraska's Republican legislators have since redrawn the Second Congressional District to make it harder for a Democrat to win there in the future.)

The District Plan has five drawbacks. First, the plan would encourage regional and probably extreme minor parties. A third-party candidate wouldn't need to win a whole state to affect an election. He or she could build a block of electoral votes instead simply by winning a few extreme right-wing or left-wing congressional districts, and this would greatly increase the chance of an electoral deadlock.

Second, the District Plan would push state legislatures to gerrymander congressional districts even more baldly than they do already. (Gerrymandering means packing the voters who favor a different party into a few throwaway districts, so that your party can win many more districts by close margins.) In 2012, the Democrats took 50.4% of the total vote in the nation's races for the US House of Representatives, yet won only 46.2% of the seats in the legislative body. Republican gerrymandering in 2011, following their state legislative victories in 2010, successfully prevented the Democrats from turning their nationwide majority of votes in 2012 into a legislative majority in the US House in 2013 and 2014. Under the District Plan, with the presidency at stake, gerrymandering would probably become even more brazen.

The District Plan's third defect is that it could lead to dozens of recounts in closely fought congressional districts across the nation, making the legal disputes in Florida in 2000 seem few and limited by comparison.

Fourth, unless all 50 states adopt the District Plan at the same time, the states that use the plan first will suffer a loss of power relative to the states that continue to use winner-take-all. If, for example, Pennsylvania adopted the District Plan, and its 18 congressional districts were evenly divided between the two major presidential candidates, the state's total vote would be split: 11 electoral votes for the candidate who won the state and 9 for his opponent, a margin between the winner and loser of only 2 electoral votes. By contrast, if Delaware were still using the winner-take-all system, it would continue to award all 3 of its electoral votes to the candidate who wins the state and none to the candidate who loses, a margin between the winner and loser in the state of 3 electoral votes. Under the District Plan, Pennsylvania could have even less influence in a national election than Delaware.

Fifth and most important, the District Plan would create an even greater discrepancy between the popular vote and the electoral vote than the current system does. Many urban congressional districts have minority groups that routinely favor presidential candidates by margins of 10 to 1 or more, and many rural districts also favor candidates by lopsided margins. Under the District Plan, these votes would be wasted because each congressional district would have just one electoral vote no matter how big or small a presidential candidate's margin of victory there is. "Swing states" would be replaced by "swing districts," mostly in the suburbs. Farmers, southerners, Blacks, and Latinos who live in congressional districts where one party is dominant would continue to be ignored.

Even in an election as close as the one in 2000, only one-eighth of the nation's congressional districts were competitive, so the campaigns that year would have ignored seven-eighths of the American people. And George W. Bush would have won even more electoral votes in 2000 under the District Plan than he did under the current system—288 instead of 271. The District Plan would also have made Richard Nixon victorious in 1960, with Nixon winning 279 electoral votes to John Kennedy's 242 (with 14 electoral votes for Virginia Senator Harry Byrd) even though Nixon won slightly fewer popular votes than Kennedy. The District Plan would also have led to a 269–269 tie in the electoral vote in 1976 between Gerald Ford and the popular-vote winner, Jimmy Carter.

The bias of the District Plan toward Republican candidates and against cities was particularly clear in 2012, when President Obama won popular-vote majorities in four of the most populous states—Michigan, Pennsylvania, Virginia, and Ohio—but thanks to severe Republican gerrymandering the year before, lost 41 of their 59 congressional districts. Under the District Plan, President Obama would have received only 26 of these four states' 67 electoral votes (instead of taking all 67 under the winner-take-all system).

Across the nation in 2012, the District Plan would have given 276 electoral votes to Mitt Romney, even though Romney received only 47% of the popular vote, and only 262 electoral votes to President Obama, although he won 51% of the popular vote.

Before the District Plan can even begin to be considered, we need to have fair, nonpartisan, and non-gerrymandered congressional districts in all 50 states.

Four States If the District Plan Had Been Used in 2012

State	Obama's % of the Popular Vote	Actual Electoral Vote	Congressional District Victories	District Plan Electoral Vote
Michigan	54%	Obama 16, Romney 0	Romney 9, Obama 5	Romney 9, Obama 7
Pennsylvania	52%	Obama 20, Romney 0	Romney 13, Obama 5	Romney 13, Obama 7
Virginia	51%	Obama 13, Romney 0	Romney 7, Obama 4	Romney 7, Obama 6
Ohio	50.7%	Obama 18, Romney 0	Romney 12, Obama 4	Romney 12, Obama 6

Proportional Representation

A third alternative to the electoral system is proportional representation, favored at different times by Alexis de Tocqueville, John Stuart Mill, Franklin Roosevelt, and Robert Kennedy. In a presidential election under proportional representation, each candidate who has won 5% or more of a state's popular vote would receive a fractional share of the state's electoral votes too. If proportional representation had been in effect in 2012, Mitt Romney would have won 20 of California's 55 electoral votes in 2012, and Barack Obama would have taken 16 of Texas's 38 electoral votes. Supporters of a candidate who finished second in a state would finally have some of their state's electoral votes go to someone who they voted *for*.

The great advantage of proportional representation is that it would empower many groups who have long been ignored under the winner-take-all system, such as conservatives in New York and liberals in Texas, because even in states with lopsided one-party majorities, every vote would count. Proportional representation would prevent votes from being wasted, as so many votes are under the winner-take-all system, because everyone would become a swing voter, not just moderates in the battleground states. Under proportional representation, if 49% of the people in a state voted for a losing candidate, the candidate would receive 49% (or nearly that) of the state's electoral vote too.

Proportional representation would greatly favor the small states, however, because it would replace the winner-take-all system that benefits the populous states, but leave intact the two-extra-electors distortion that favors the sparsely populated states. Not surprisingly, when the US Senate voted in 1950 for a constitutional amendment to establish proportional representation, the Rules Committee in the House of Representatives, where many members represented big cities, blocked the resolution from even coming to a vote.

In Europe, 18 nations use proportional representation to elect their parliaments. So do Australia, New Zealand, Japan, Chile, South Africa, and Israel. (In Israel, where right-wing religious parties have a disproportionate influence, it is not because of proportional representation, but because an Israeli political party needs only 2% of the vote to win seats in parliament.)

In several nations, proportional representation gives racial minorities some long overdue representation. When New Zealand adopted proportional representation in 1996, for example, the native Maoris tripled their numbers in parliament. Proportional representation has also enabled South Africa's whites to win 20% of the seats in parliament, while a system with only one representative per district would have left them with almost none. John Stuart Mill, the great political philosopher, would have approved. In his 1861 book, *Representative Government*, Mill wrote, "It is an essential part of every democracy that minorities should be adequately represented . . . nothing but a false show of democracy is possible without it."

In fact, the one-representative-per-district system, which makes it difficult for minorities to win representation, is a 19th-century, largely Anglo-Saxon anachronism. Only Britain, France, Nepal, and five of Britain's former colonies—the United States, Canada, India, Pakistan, and Jamaica—still use this method of voting to determine who represents a legislative district. Indeed, Britain elected a second-place prime minister in 1974, when the Labour Party, led by Harold Wilson, won 1% fewer votes across Britain than the Conservative Party did, but still won three more seats in parliament.

~

The worst drawback of proportional representation is that it makes third-party candidacies easier. This is fine in parliamentary elections, when third- and fourth-party candidates can sometimes take more nuanced positions on the issues. By contrast, two-party systems reward mud-slinging and obstructionism, because if one party succeeds in creating discontent with the other, the voters have nowhere else to go. In a two-party system, the only alternative voters have to an incumbent is a candidate from the very same party that made it hard for the incumbent to govern well in the first place.

But in an American presidential election, proportional representation would make it much easier for a third-party candidate to prevent anyone else from winning a majority of the electoral vote. Then, under

Article II of the Constitution, the House of Representatives would vote for president using the grossly unfair one-state-one-vote method described earlier. Yet even before this antiquated vote would take place, a third-party candidate would try to negotiate with one or both of the major-party candidates during the six weeks in between Election Day and the Monday in December when the electors actually cast their votes. This period could easily become a time for competitive offers and secret deals, as the public, with little control over the outcome, would grow increasingly cynical.

In 2000, proportional representation would have allowed Ralph Nader, who won only 2.7% of the vote nationwide, to win two electoral votes in California and one electoral vote each in nine other states. Nader's 11 electoral votes would have denied both George W. Bush and Al Gore an electoral-vote majority, and ensured that the presidential election that year would have been decided either by a shady deal between the candidates in December or a one-state-one-vote circus in the House of Representatives in January. In 1992, proportional representation would also have allowed Ross Perot to deny an electoral majority to Bill Clinton.

In fact, in 10 of the last 35 presidential elections, proportional representation would have made an electoral majority impossible, and each of these elections might then have been decided either by a backroom deal in December or a Wyoming-equals-California farce in the House of Representatives in January. Proportional representation works well in Europe, but in an American presidential election, because the House of Representatives still decides deadlocked elections with a one-state-one-vote ballot, it would be a disaster.

With a little tweaking, however, proportional representation can make our electoral system fairer without helping third-party candidates impose deadlocks. If the presidential candidate who wins the most popular votes in a state could take only *one-third* of the state's electoral votes rather than all of them, and if the rest of the state's electoral votes were proportionally divided *only between the state's top two vote-winners*, our electoral system could be fairer without becoming more dangerous. (Much more about this "Winner-Takes-Most" reform later, in chapters 9 and 10.)

But proportional representation as it is usually proposed, where a third-party candidate with only a small percentage of the popular vote can nonetheless win many electoral votes, is simply too risky in America.

National Popular Vote

A fourth and new way of electing presidents, National Popular Vote, has already been adopted by 10 states: California, New York, Illinois, New Jersey, Massachusetts, Washington, Maryland, Hawaii, Rhode Island, and Vermont, as well as the District of Columbia. The reform has also been approved at various times by the state senates of Maine, North Carolina, Oklahoma, and Colorado, and by the lower legislative houses in eight other states.

Under the National Popular Vote system, states agree in advance to give their electoral votes to whoever wins the most popular votes nationwide, but the system will not take effect until all the participating states together have 270 electoral votes, a majority of the nation's total. In a presidential election year, no state can withdraw from the National Popular Vote compact during a six-month "blackout period" between July 20 and January 20 of the following year. This period includes the party conventions, the national campaign, Election Day, the vote by the 538 electors in their 50 state capitals, the counting of the electoral votes by Congress, and Inauguration Day.

Conceived in 2001 by Robert Bennett, a law professor at Northwestern University, National Popular Vote makes an end run around the difficult process of amending the Constitution. In effect, it replaces the electoral system with direct elections—getting rid of swing states and runner-up presidents—without having to win the support of two-thirds of Congress and three-fourths of the state legislatures.

California's state legislature was the first to pass National Popular Vote in 2006, but Governor Arnold Schwarzenegger vetoed the measure. Five years later, both houses of California's legislature passed it again, and this time Governor Jerry Brown signed the bill into law. Although California's 55 electoral votes are reliably Democratic and the National Popular Vote system could easily swing these votes to the Republicans, few Republicans voted for the measure. For now, most Republicans support the status quo because they benefited from our electoral system's pro-rural bias in the 2000 election, and don't realize just how strong the system's pro-urban bias is too (because of the winner-take-all format).

National Popular Vote would be fine if it could work. Unfortunately, the reform's end run around the Constitution is also its great weakness. Because the National Popular Vote system is only a *contract* rather than a constitutional requirement, the power to enforce it is extremely weak. Suppose, for example, that Sarah Palin is leading slightly in a future three-way race for president. Will the people of New York, Illinois, and California really sit by and meekly give her all of their electoral votes? Or will the legislatures in these states rush to withdraw from the compact, blackout period be damned? Conservatives would surely file a lawsuit to prevent such a withdrawal, and the case would quickly go to the Supreme Court.

Do we really want the Supreme Court to decide another election? And do it in a hurry again to avoid the nightmare of not having a president-elect ready to be inaugurated by January 20? Because despite the best intentions, this is precisely where National Popular Vote will take us.

Defenders of the National Popular Vote system have argued that states would be unable to withdraw from the compact during an election year's blackout period because even if a state's legislators did vote to breach their contract and withdraw, laws usually take some time before they become effective. But in 44 states and the District of Columbia, the legislatures can specify the effective date of any law they pass, and in four of the remaining states, they can pass emergency legislation to allow a law to take effect immediately. Only in Texas and West Virginia must 90 days pass (unless there is a two-thirds vote) before a law can take force, but even a 90-day delay would allow either state to withdraw from the National Popular Vote compact as late as mid-September and still resume control over how the state would cast its electoral votes in mid-December.

In some states, lawsuits claiming that the National Popular Vote system violates the 1965 Voting Rights Act would also be likely. In California, for example, about 30% of the voters are Latino, and under the National Popular Vote compact, they would completely lose their enormous influence over how the state's 55 electoral votes are awarded. Similar lawsuits over the loss of a minority group's influence could also be filed in New Mexico, the District of Columbia, and Hawaii.

Still another problem with National Popular Vote is that so far only Democratic states have joined the compact. If this trend continues, and one or two swing states join too so that the National Popular Vote system can actually take effect, there could be a period where the Democratic states have promised to cast their electoral votes for whoever wins the most popular votes, even a Republican, while the Republican states would not have made any such promise in return. During this time there could never be a Democratic runner-up president, because the Democratic states would be giving their electoral votes to a Republican rather than a second-place Democrat (and any Republican candidate during this period who won the popular vote by even a slight margin would also win the electoral vote by a landslide).

By contrast, if a Republican candidate won fewer popular votes than his or her Democratic rival, he or she could still eke out a narrow victory in the electoral vote if he or she finished first in one of the states that joined the National Popular Vote compact and then sued, successfully, for that state's electoral votes.

❧

Is the National Popular Vote pact enforceable? After all, interstate compacts have governed activities from river dredging to multistate lottery tickets, and defenders of the National Popular Vote system cite several cases where federal courts have ordered one state to fulfill its contractual duty to another. But in a number of disputes where a state has breached a contract, it is easier for a court to order the state to pay damages than it is to force the state to stay in a compact against its will.

Nebraska, for example, joined the Central Interstate Low Level Radioactive Waste Compact in 1983, along with Kansas, Oklahoma, Arkansas, and Louisiana. The five states jointly disposed of radioactively contaminated tools, clothing, filters, and equipment from nuclear power plants. In 1989 the states agreed to deposit their low-level waste at a new disposal site in Boyd County, in north-central Nebraska. But in 1998, after a decade of determined resistance by Boyd County's residents, Nebraska's state government had second thoughts and denied a license to the utilities that the five states had hired to build the depository. The next year Nebraska withdrew from the compact altogether.

The four other states sued, claiming that Nebraska had acted in bad faith, and won their case both in federal district court and in the US Court of Appeals for the Eighth Circuit. Finally, in 2005, six years after Nebraska's withdrawal from the compact, the state paid seven utilities from the other four states $145.8 million in damages, an amount equal to $83 per Nebraska resident. Nebraska had to pay damages for withdrawing from the interstate radioactive waste compact, but it did not have to rejoin the compact or build the hated waste disposal site.

This is the problem with contract law: *Money can be a substitute for performance.* Suppose New York and California decide to withdraw from the National Popular Vote compact one month before an election. How many liberal Democrats wouldn't gladly pay $83 or an equivalent amount in damages to prevent Sarah Palin from becoming president? The idea behind the National Popular Vote reform is admirable, but the compact itself is unenforceable, and it would lead to political, and soon judicial, chaos.

A final problem with the National Popular Vote compact is that many voters would be confused about who they were voting for. Suppose that in a future election Massachusetts Senator Elizabeth Warren is leading in the national polls, and a Republican voter who lives in a state that has joined the National Popular Vote compact wants to vote against her. What is he or she to do? If the state's electoral votes will go to Warren no matter who wins the popular vote in this voter's individual state, he or she would effectively have no way to vote for any Republican electors, and might as well stay home (or alternatively, file a lawsuit).

Similarly, if Rand Paul is leading in the national polls, a Democrat, even in a liberal state, might have no effective way to vote for any Democratic electors. For this reason alone, the constitutionality of the National Popular Vote system is uncertain. The Constitution gives state legislatures the power to say *how* electors will be chosen, not *for whom* the electors will vote.

The burden of proof that a reform is worthwhile is on those who propose the untested alternative, because changing the rules of an election also means changing the tasks and the strategy that a candidate must pursue to win. In the 1970s, for example, when the Democratic and Republican national committees took the power to choose convention delegates away from their state party bosses by increasing the number of presidential primaries, it eventually led to a front-loading of early primaries on "Super Tuesdays" in February, and to an enormous lengthening of the presidential primary campaign season. Primaries are still a better way to choose presidents than boss-led smoke-filled rooms, but the decision in the 1970s to increase the number of primaries has had several unintended consequences, including the strengthening of the Republican party's right wing and the Democratic Party's left wing.

Because reforming our electoral-vote system also runs the risk of unintended consequences, possibly including new and extreme political parties, more electoral deadlocks, and an increase in hasty Supreme Court decisions, the Constitution should be amended only with extreme caution. Unfortunately, all of the previously suggested alternatives to the electoral system have been too sweeping. None of the proposed reforms seems limited enough and safe enough to win the support of the two-thirds of the Congress and three-fourths of the state legislatures required for a constitutional amendment, nor does National Popular Vote seem likely to win the support of an additional 15 or 20 state legislatures.

SWING STATES

For more than 200 years, our electoral system has forced presidential candidates to concentrate on winning swing states, but not one of the most widely considered changes to the electoral system—direct elections, the District Plan, proportional representation, or National Popular Vote—gives swing states the slightest role. Yet without the support of some of them, it is doubtful that any reform will ever be approved by enough state legislatures to ratify a constitutional amendment, because it takes only 13 states to block an amendment's ratification.

Swing states receive all of the attention during a presidential campaign because their voters are evenly divided between the Republicans and Democrats, so their blocks of electoral votes can be won by either party. Currently, there are 11 swing states:

West	Midwest	South	Northeast
Colorado	Ohio	Florida	Pennsylvania
Nevada	Michigan	Virginia	New Hampshire
	Wisconsin	North Carolina	
	Iowa		

Swing states change from decade to decade. A generation ago, California, Illinois, and New Jersey were swing states, and Florida, Colorado, and Virginia were not. Despite this fluidity, a state that is currently competitive will not want to change the electoral system when it receives so much attention from the candidates and the parties.

Three-fourths of the campaign visits that Barack Obama and John McCain made in 2008 took place in only seven states, and half of their visits went to just three: Ohio, Florida, and Pennsylvania. By contrast, California, Texas, and New York had few visits, almost no television commercials, and hardly a yard sign.* Understandably, voter turnout in the 39 "spectator" states is usually 7% to 9% lower than it is in the 11 swing states, and sometimes lower still.

In 2012, campaign visits were even more highly concentrated than they were in 2008. During the last two months of the 2012 campaign, 96% of the campaign visits (as opposed to fundraisers) by Barack Obama, Mitt Romney, Joe Biden, and Paul Ryan were paid to only eight states, and 59% of their visits went to just three states: Ohio, Florida, and Virginia.

---

* In 1999 New York Senator Charles Schumer proposed that New York and Texas put their electoral votes together to create a super-swing state with a massive bloc of 65 electoral votes, which would have guaranteed repeated visits by the candidates to the two states. At the time, New York, a Democratic state, and Texas, a Republican state, had almost the same number of electoral votes and the same margin of victory, 60% to 40%, by their dominant political party. Today, however, the pool is no longer possible because Texas has 38 electoral votes, while New York has only 29.

Similarly, in 2000, Florida and Ohio each endured more than 28,000 political television commercials, and even West Virginia, a much smaller state, suffered nearly 15,000. By contrast, the Bush and Gore campaigns completely ignored big cities such as New York, Washington, Houston, Dallas, Atlanta, Phoenix, and Denver, and the Gore campaign also did not spend a dime on media in Los Angeles or San Francisco. Among the 30 least populous states in 2000, Bush, Gore, Cheney, and Lieberman paid more visits to the swing states of Iowa and New Mexico than they did to all of the other 28 states combined.

It was the same in 2008. Ninety-nine percent of the campaign advertising during the last six weeks of the campaign took place in only 16 states, effectively eliminating the other 34 states (and 65% of the American people) from the campaign. Half of the television advertisements were broadcast in just three states: Ohio, Pennsylvania, and especially Florida, which put up with more than 50,000 separate broadcasts of campaign commercials.

Advertising was even more intense in 2012, but once again half of the campaign commercials were broadcast in just three states: Florida, Ohio, and Virginia. Cleveland's viewers alone endured nearly 75,000 political ads that year.

———

Many people have written that the largest urban areas play a greater role in our electoral system than they actually do. They mistakenly think that the winner-take-all system increases the power of city-dwellers such as Catholics, Blacks, Latinos, Jews, and union members because these groups live in populous urban states with big, strategic blocs of electoral votes. Senator John Kennedy, for example, opposed a bill for direct presidential elections in 1956 because he believed that the winner-take-all system counterbalanced the exaggerated weight that small states have possessed with their equal representation in the US Senate and their two extra electoral votes per state in presidential elections. With Kennedy's help, the 1956 Senate bill for direct elections was defeated, 63 to 28.

While it is true that the winner-take-all system can be a boon to some urban groups, the key factor is not whether the voters live in a big

state or a small state, but whether they live in a swing state or a spectator state. Swing state voters such as Cubans in Florida, union workers
in Ohio, and coal miners in Pennsylvania have a political influence far
beyond their numbers. By contrast, Jews in New York and California are
powerful only because of their financial contributions; their actual votes
in these heavily Democratic states have little effect on a national election's
outcome. And while Latino voters in Florida, Colorado, and Nevada have
enormous influence in a national campaign, the many more Hispanics
who live in California, Texas, and New York do not.

For decades, many liberals have also incorrectly thought that the
winner-take-all system helps Blacks because most Blacks live in populous
states rather than small states. But even today, more Blacks live in the
South than in the northern cities, and the 10-to-1 majorities that Blacks
in Texas, Alabama, and other southern states commonly give to Democratic candidates for president are wasted because these states usually go
Republican. In the North and West, equally lopsided Democratic majorities among Blacks in New York, Illinois, and California have also counted
for little in a presidential campaign, because these states are already reliably Democratic.

The idea that the winner-take-all system helps urban minorities and
ethnic groups is a myth because most urban voters live in uncontested
"spectator" states such as California, Texas, New York, and Georgia, states
that are repeatedly ignored during presidential campaigns. But it is also
a myth that America's electoral system helps the smallest states (each of
which has two more electoral votes than its sparse population warrants)
because unless the small state is also a swing state, it receives almost no
visits from a presidential candidate during a national campaign.

For almost two centuries, the real beneficiaries of the winner-take-all
system have been the blue-collar whites (and some minorities) who live
in an arc of northern "heartland" states that extends from Pennsylvania
to Iowa, a region which has also recently leapfrogged west to include
Colorado and Nevada, and south to include Virginia, North Carolina,
and Florida. In these (currently) 11 swing states, the percentage of Blacks
living in Virginia, North Carolina, and Michigan is higher than the percentage of Blacks nationwide, but the percentage of Blacks in the other

eight states is lower than the national average, and the proportion of Blacks is particularly low in Colorado, Wisconsin, and Iowa. Most voters in the heartland states live in small cities and towns rather than big ones, and for the most part they are older, more homogenous, and slightly less educated than the nation as a whole.

Any reform of the nation's electoral system, if it is to have even a slim chance of passing, should not only preserve the balance of power between urban and rural states, it must also preserve some of the power of the millions of blue-collar Americans who live in the swing states. Otherwise the congressmen and state legislators who represent them will never agree to the change.

CHAPTER 9

How Barack Obama Nearly Became a Runner-Up President

The Search for a More Perfect Electoral System

EVEN THE LUCKY SWING-STATE VOTERS WHO BENEFIT FROM OUR electoral system—retirees in Florida, union workers in Ohio, farmers in Iowa—don't really want someone to win a presidential election with fewer popular votes than his or her opponent. Americans, whether they are right-wing or left-wing, want what is best for their country, and the nasty political climate that will accompany the next runner-up president will make the success of his or her administration improbable, and perhaps impossible.

Electoral reform is extremely unlikely now, but the moment a second-place president is elected again, it will immediately become a heated emotional issue, so it would help to start thinking about electoral reform now, while the prospect for change seems remote and passions are still cool. We are fortunate that the odds of electing another runner-up president can be greatly reduced with only small changes to our present system, and in the long run, the electoral system can only be preserved if it is repaired.

Of course, even a slight change in the electoral system means amending the Constitution, something almost impossible to do. Many people agree with New York's late senator, Daniel Moynihan, a liberal who nevertheless staunchly opposed electoral reform. "Leave the Constitution be," he said. "The time to consider such a measure as this will be upon us. But let us wait until its necessity is plain."

Unfortunately, by the time a reform's necessity is plain, it will be too late, because we will be stuck with another runner-up president for four years. The need to reform our electoral system became clear in 2000, when George W. Bush won the presidency with fewer popular votes than Al Gore. The election that year, to borrow a phrase from Thomas Jefferson, was "like a fire-bell in the night."

How to Make Our Elections Safer

We don't have to get rid of electoral votes to make them safer. Because our electoral system has two arithmetical biases that distort an election's outcome, two reforms can cut these quirks in half and make the chance of electing another second-place president *four* times less likely. And the reforms can do this without altering the balance of power between urban and rural states, without changing the state-by-state nature of presidential campaigns, and without ending the role of the swing states.

First: Give each state only one electoral vote more than its population warrants, instead of two, as is the case now, by taking one electoral vote away from every state. Wyoming and Vermont would each have 2 electoral votes instead of 3, and California would have 54 electoral votes instead of 55.

Then, to balance this *enormous* concession by the small states: Award only a *minority* of a state's electoral votes on a winner-take-all basis. Award the *majority* of the state's electoral votes *in proportion* to the number of popular votes that the state's top two (and only the top two) candidates won in the state. States would no longer have to give all of their electoral votes to just one candidate. They could instead award most of their votes to the candidate who finished first in the state, but some of their votes to the candidate who came in second.

This simple pair of reforms can make our electoral system safer by making runner-up presidencies much less likely, but first we need to ask two important questions:

1. How many of a state's electoral votes should be awarded on a winner-take-all basis?
2. How many of a state's electoral votes should be divided proportionally?

The Similarity between the 1888 and 2012 Elections

A path to answering these two questions appeared in 2012, when the presidential election that year turned out to be remarkably similar to the contest in 1888, when Benjamin Harrison defeated President Grover Cleveland even though he won 90,000 fewer popular votes than Cleveland.

Look at the maps of these two elections and much is the same, except that today Florida and Virginia often align with the North, while most of the Great Plains aligns with the South. More important, in both 1888 and 2012 the presidential candidate favored by the urban, industrial North had a large, built-in advantage in the electoral vote. This makes the 2012 election quite different from the contest in 2000, when the electoral system's pro-rural bias helped the candidate favored by the Great Plains and Rocky Mountain states.

In 1888 the Democratic candidate, President Grover Cleveland, won more than 65% of the popular vote in every Deep South state except Florida (and even there, he won 59% of the vote), while in the northern states the Republican candidate, Benjamin Harrison, barely defeated Cleveland in Ohio (by only 2%), New York (by 1%), and Indiana (by just ½ of 1%). The small size of Harrison's leads in these states did not matter; what counted was that Harrison won them. Together, these three swing states gave him 74 electoral votes, more than his margin of victory over Cleveland.

Similarly, in 2012 Mitt Romney won landslides of 57% of the vote or more in 15 southern, Great Plains, and Rocky Mountain states, but President Obama won all of the northern and western swing states (Pennsylvania, Ohio, Wisconsin, New Hampshire, Iowa, Colorado, and Nevada) by relatively narrow margins of between 3% and 7%. Again, the small size of Obama's leads in these states did not matter—it was enough that he won them. Together, these seven swing states gave President Obama 73 electoral votes, and without them he would have fallen 11 votes short of the 270 that he needed to be reelected president.

But even if Governor Romney had won another 2.44 million votes and led Obama nationally in the popular vote by a half a percentage point—the same popular-vote margin by which Al Gore led George W.

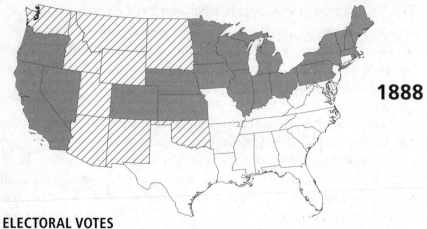

1888

ELECTORAL VOTES

Harrison	▓	233	47.8% Pop. Vote
Cleveland	☐	168	48.6% Pop. Vote
Territories	▨		

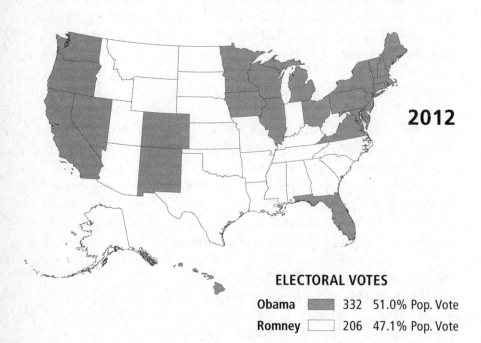

2012

ELECTORAL VOTES

Obama	▓	332	51.0% Pop. Vote
Romney	☐	206	47.1% Pop. Vote

Bush in 2000—it would not have been enough for Romney to win the presidency. More precisely, if Romney had won 2.2% more of the popular vote in every state, and President Obama had won 2.2% less of the popular vote in every state, the nation's popular vote would have been Romney 49.35%, Obama 48.81%, but Romney still would have lost the election. Romney would have won Florida and Virginia, but among the northern and western swing states, he would have taken only Ohio. So even if Romney had won the nation's popular vote by half a percentage point, he would have lost the electoral vote to President Obama, 272 to 266.

In 2000 the electoral math favored the rural states and the Republicans, but in 2012 it favored the industrial states and the Democrats. To win the nation's popular vote in 2012, Mitt Romney needed another 1.93% of the vote, but to win the *electoral* vote and the presidency, he needed an additional 2.7% of the popular vote. In between, if Romney had won anywhere from 1.93% more to 2.69% more of the popular vote in each state than he did—a range of ¾ of 1% of the vote, which in a close election is an enormous spread—then Barack Obama would have been a runner-up president during his second term, just as George W. Bush was during his first term.

THE SEARCH FOR A POLITICALLY NEUTRAL REPAIR

The good news this predicament offers is that we now have an excellent test for determining whether an electoral reform is politically neutral:

- Is there a numerical format for awarding electoral votes that would have allowed both Al Gore to win in 2000 and Mitt Romney to win in 2012, if Romney had won an extra 2.2% of the popular vote in every state at Obama's expense (and led President Obama in the popular vote by ½ of 1%, the same margin that Gore enjoyed)?

How should this search begin? To start, what if a state's popular-vote winner could only take 40% of a state's electoral votes before the rest of the state's votes were divided proportionally? Could a "Winner-Takes-40%"

format* reduce the power of the northern swing states enough to make an electoral system politically neutral? Unfortunately, no. Even with an extra 2.2% of the popular vote, Romney would still have lost the 2012 election to President Obama under a Winner-Takes-40% system: 244 electoral votes to 243.[†]

By contrast, under a "Winner-Takes-25%" format,[‡] Romney would have won in 2012 (if he had received 2.2% more of the popular vote), 244 electoral votes to 243. But under the same format in 2000, Bush would have beaten Gore, 244 electoral votes to 243, so the Winner-Takes-25% system is not politically neutral either, because it reduces the power of the northern swing states a little too much.

(By the way, if the hypothetical election margins here seem razor-thin, it is because the results *should* be razor-thin for elections as close as the actual contest in 2000 or the hypothetical election in 2012 if Romney had won an extra 2.2% of the popular vote.)

Fortunately, better results come when the winner of a state's popular vote takes between 30% and 35% of the state's electoral votes before the rest of the state's votes are divided proportionally between the state's top two vote-winners.

Three electoral formats seem to be politically neutral:

---

* i.e., rounding the winner of a state's 40% share of the electoral votes *down* to the next whole number before the rest of the state's electoral votes are divided proportionally between the state's top two popular-vote winners. In California, for example, 40% of the state's 54 electoral votes (55 minus 1) is 21.6, so rounding down, 21 electoral votes would go to the winner of the state's popular vote, and 33 electoral votes would be divided proportionally according to the votes won by the state's top two candidates. In 2012, under the Winner-Takes-40% format, the state's result would have been Obama 42, Romney 12.

† Because every state and the District of Columbia would have one less electoral vote than before, the national total of electoral votes under this reform would be 487 rather than 538, and a candidate would need only 244 electoral votes to win the presidency instead of 270.

‡ i.e., rounding the winner of a state's 25% share of the electoral votes *up* to the next whole number before the rest of the state's electoral votes are divided proportionally between the state's top two popular-vote winners. In California, for example, 25% of the state's 54 electoral votes (55 minus 1) is 13.5, so rounding up, 14 electoral votes would go to the winner of the state's popular vote, and 40 electoral votes would be divided proportionally. In 2012, under a Winner-Takes-25% system, the state's result would have been Obama 39, Romney 15.

- Winner-Takes-35% (rounding *down*)*
- Winner-Takes-1/3 (rounding to the *nearest* whole number)†
- Winner-Takes-30% (rounding *up*)‡

The chart on the next page shows how these three promising formats would have awarded our nation's electoral votes in 1876, 1888, and 2000, as well as in 2012 if Romney had won an extra 2.2% of the popular vote at Obama's expense.

All three of these formulas would have allowed Al Gore to win in 2000, Samuel Tilden to win in 1876, and Mitt Romney—if he had won an extra 2.2% of the popular vote in each state at Obama's expense—to win in 2012, though none of these formulas would have enabled Grover Cleveland to beat Benjamin Harrison in 1888.

Still, Winner-Takes-1/3 (rounding to the nearest whole number) appears to be even more politically neutral than the other formats, because the margins of victory that it gives to Al Gore in 2000 and Mitt Romney in 2012 are identical, which is not true of the other two formulas.

Winner-Takes-1/3 is not only the easiest of the three formulas to understand, it would also have provided the best result in the 1888 election. The 1888 presidential election, despite its similarity to the contest

---

* i.e., rounding the winner of a state's 35% share of the electoral votes *down* to the next whole number (with a minimum of one electoral vote) before the rest of the state's electoral votes are divided proportionally between the state's top two popular-vote winners. In California, for example, 35% of the state's 54 electoral votes (55 minus 1) is 18.9, so rounding down, 18 electoral votes would go to the winner of the state's popular vote, and 36 electoral votes would be divided proportionally. In 2012 the statewide total would have been Obama 40, Romney 14.

† i.e., rounding the winner of a state's 1/3 share of the electoral votes to the *nearest* whole number (with a minimum of one electoral vote) before the rest of the state's electoral votes are divided proportionally between the state's top two popular-vote winners. In California, for example, 1/3 of 54 electoral votes is 18, so rounding to the nearest whole number, 18 electoral votes would go to the winner of the state's popular vote, and 36 electoral votes would be divided proportionally. In 2012 the statewide total would have been Obama 40, Romney 14.

‡ i.e., rounding the winner of a state's 30% share of the electoral votes *up* to the next whole number before the rest of the state's electoral votes are divided proportionally between the state's top two candidates. In California, for example, 30% of 54 electoral votes is 16.2, so rounding up, 17 electoral votes would go to the winner of the state's popular vote, and 37 electoral votes would be divided proportionally. In 2012 the statewide total would have been Obama 40, Romney 14.

Election Results under the Most Promising Formats

Format Used	2012 Hypothetical (Romney +2.2%, Obama -2.2%)	2000	1888	1876
Current Winner-Take-All System	Obama 272 Romney 266	Bush 271 Gore 266	Harrison 233 Cleveland 168	Hayes 185 Tilden 184
Winner-Takes-35% (Rounding Down)	Romney 245 Obama 242	Gore 246 Bush 241	Harrison 189 Cleveland 174	Tilden 167 Hayes 164
Winner-Takes-1/3 (Rounding to Nearest Whole Number)	Romney 245 Obama 242	Gore 245 Bush 242	Harrison 184 Cleveland 179	Tilden 169 Hayes 162
Winner-Takes-30% (Rounding Up)	Romney 246 Obama 241	Gore 245 Bush 242	Harrison 186 Cleveland 177	Tilden 171 Hayes 160

in 2012, is an outlier. Benjamin Harrison won New York, Indiana, and Ohio and their 74 electoral votes by tiny margins, while Grover Cleveland racked up huge 82% and 74% majorities in South Carolina and Mississippi that only won him 18 electoral votes. Despite President Cleveland's lead in the nation's popular vote, 48.6% to 47.8%, Harrison won a big electoral victory, 233 to 168, a decisive margin of 65 electoral votes. By contrast, George W. Bush defeated Al Gore in 2000 by only five electoral votes, and Rutherford B. Hayes beat Samuel Tilden in 1876 by just one vote.

Because Harrison's lead of 65 electoral votes in 1888 was so large, the goal of finding an electoral formula that would have allowed the popular-vote winner, Grover Cleveland, to overcome Harrison's lead and win the electoral vote too may be impossible. But to insist that an electoral reform work flawlessly in every past election is to make the perfect the enemy of the good. The right thing to do is not to give up, but to find the best electoral format we can, and not fret too much about how well the reform might or might not have worked in 1888. Indeed, if you had set South Carolina and Mississippi apart from the rest of the country in 1888 (and these two states were riddled with Jim Crow–era injustices), it is Benjamin Harrison who won the popular vote in America's 36 other states, so perhaps Harrison deserved to win 1888's election after all.

Once we stop worrying about whether an electoral formula could have let Grover Cleveland win the election in 1888, we can take another look at the three most promising electoral systems. Winner-Takes-1/3 is not only the most politically neutral reform and the easiest one to grasp, it also would have reduced Harrison's 65-electoral-vote margin of victory in 1888 to *just 5 votes*. So keeping in mind aesthetics, political neutrality, and the test of how well a formula works in past elections, the Winner-Takes-1/3 formula is the best way to make our electoral system safer without changing the balance of power between the urban states and rural states.

Here is the **Winner-Takes-1/3** reform, expressed in full:

The number of electoral votes a state possesses shall be equal to the number of members a state has in the US House of Representatives, plus one (i.e., **every state shall have one less electoral vote than it did**

before),* and the number of electoral votes that the District of Columbia has shall continue to be equal to that of the least populous state.

And, during a presidential election, **the winner of a state's popular vote for president,** and the winner of a state's popular vote for vice president, **shall take only one-third of the state's electoral votes on a winner-take-all basis** (rounding fractions of electoral votes to the *nearest* whole number, but never rounding below a minimum of one electoral vote), **and the state's remaining electoral votes shall be divided proportionally between the state's top two popular-vote winners,** in accordance with the number of popular votes that they won in the state.

⁓

In no case under Winner-Takes-1/3 would the winner of a state's popular vote ever receive less than *two-thirds* of the state's electoral votes, because the popular-vote winner would not only receive one-third of the state's electoral votes to start with, he or she would also take at least half of the state's remaining electoral votes as well.

Under the Winner-Takes-1/3 system in 2000, for example, Florida would have had 24 electoral votes instead of 25. One-third of them (8 electoral votes) would have been awarded to George W. Bush to start with because he won the state's popular vote (officially, Florida's percentages were Bush 48.85%, Gore 48.84%), while the remaining 16 electoral votes would have been divided proportionally, in this case by an 8-to-8 split between Bush and Gore. Florida's total electoral vote therefore would have been Bush 16, Gore 8, so Bush would have taken two-thirds of the evenly divided state's 24 electoral votes.†

---

* It is important that the number of electoral votes each state has be only *one* more than its population warrants, instead of *two* more, as is the case now. If the Winner-Takes-⅓ format is applied without subtracting an electoral vote from every state, the result in 2000 would have been Bush 270, Gore 268, and the result in 2012 (if Romney had won an extra 2.2% of the popular vote in every state at Obama's expense) would have been Obama 269, Romney 269.

† To implement the Winner-Takes-1/3 reform, parties offering statewide slates of electors will need to **rank** the people running to become electors in numerical order, so that everyone will know in advance which electors will serve and not serve when their party's candidate wins some of a state's electoral votes and not others. If Florida had used the Winner-Takes-1/3 system in 2000, for example, the first 16 of the state's 24 Republican elector-nominees pledged to Bush would have served as electors, as would the first 8 of the state's 24 Democratic elector-nominees pledged to Gore.

In fact, the Winner-Takes-1/3 system can more accurately be called *Winner-Takes-Most*. Yet the small difference in the state-by-state totals of electoral votes between the Winner-Takes-Most reform (where the electoral system's pro-urban and pro-rural distortions have been cut in half or better) and our present winner-take-all system (where the pro-urban and pro-rural biases continue undiminished) can make a runner-up presidency more than *four times less likely to happen*—without any change in the balance of power between urban and rural states, or in the state-by-state nature of presidential campaigns.

CHAPTER 10

Two Small Repairs

Winner-Takes-Most (Not All) and a Better Way to Deal with Deadlocks

WHAT DOES ALL THE ARITHMETIC IN THE LAST CHAPTER MEAN? THAT we finally have a formula for awarding electoral votes that is both safe and politically neutral.

Under the Winner-Takes-Most reform,* the winner of a state's popular vote will still take at least two-thirds of the state's electoral votes—just not all of them. Yet this small change can make a runner-up presidency four times less likely to occur.

Does the Winner-Takes-Most system require some more math? Yes,† but with computers to help us, the extra arithmetic on election night

---

* To recap chapter 9, here is the Winner-Takes-Most formula:
- Every state shall have **one less electoral vote than before.**
- During a presidential election, the winner of a state's popular vote for president (and for vice president) shall take **only one-third of the state's electoral votes on a winner-take-all basis** (rounding fractions of electoral votes to the nearest whole number, but never rounding below a minimum of one electoral vote), and **the state's remaining electoral votes shall be divided proportionally** between the state's top two popular-vote winners, rounding to whole numbers, in accordance with the number of popular votes that they won in the state.

† Do you think the Winner-Takes-Most system is complicated? Here is how the Republic of Venice—which still existed when the Founding Fathers wrote the Constitution in 1787—elected its *doge*: Thirty of the roughly 2,000 members of Venice's Great Council were chosen by lot, then reduced by a second lot to 9. The 9 members chose a new group of 40 members from the council, who then reduced themselves by lot to a group of 12, which then made a new choice of 25 council members. These 25 men reduced themselves by lot to 9, then the 9 men chose a new group of 45 council members. The 45 men were reduced by lot to 11, and it was these 11 men who finally chose the 41 members of the Great Council who would actually elect the *doge*, although a super-majority of 25 of these 41 men had to approve the final choice.

would be much less trouble than the foul political climate that could overwhelm the next second-place president. The additional math will also be less of a burden than the hard slog of permanently dealing with the extreme political parties that will inevitably form if we replace our electoral system with direct elections.

Applying the Winner-Takes-Most Reform to Past Elections

One of the most beautiful things about the Winner-Takes-Most reform is that because it *preserves* our electoral system, we can crunch numbers to see how past elections would have turned out under the reform.

In 2012, for example, California would have had 54 electoral votes under the Winner-Takes-Most format instead of the current 55, and President Obama, as the winner of the state's popular vote, would still have taken one-third of these electoral votes, or 18, as a bloc. But the other 36 electoral votes would have been divided proportionally between the state's top two popular-vote winners, Barack Obama and Mitt Romney, in accordance with the number of popular votes that they won in the state, so 22 of the proportionally divided votes would have gone for Obama and the other 14 for Romney. Then, when we add Obama's original bloc of 18 electoral votes that he won to start with, California's total electoral vote under the Winner-Takes-Most reform would have been Obama 40, Romney 14 (instead of Obama 55, Romney 0), while in Texas the electoral vote would have been Romney 27, Obama 10* (instead of Romney 38, Obama 0).

The purpose of this complexity was to prevent bribery. The stakes were high. Venetians elected a *doge* for life, but no one could ever predict with accuracy which 41 men would actually elect him. The city's convoluted system worked well for 529 years: from 1268 until Napoleon conquered Venice in May 1797, during President John Adams's third month in office.

* Texas would have had 37 electoral votes under the Winner-Takes-Most system instead of the current 38, and Romney, as the state's popular-vote winner, would have taken one-third of these electoral votes, or 12, as a bloc. The other 25 electoral votes would have been divided proportionally between the state's top two popular-vote winners, Romney and Obama, in accordance with the number of popular votes that they won in the state. So 15 of these proportionally divided votes would have gone to Romney and 10 to Obama. Then, adding Romney's initial bloc of 12 electoral votes that he won to start with, Texas's total electoral vote under the Winner-Takes-Most reform would have been Romney 27, Obama 10, instead of Romney 38, Obama 0.

Nationally, under the Winner-Takes-Most system, the electoral vote in 2012 would have been Obama 264, Romney 223, rather than the actual vote, Obama 332, Romney 206, a fairer outcome considering that Romney did win 47% of the popular vote. (Remember that with each state and the District of Columbia having one less electoral vote than before, the national total of electoral votes under the Winner-Takes-Most reform would be 487 rather than 538, and a candidate would need only 244 electoral votes to win the presidency instead of 270.)

If we look at the hypothetical election where Mitt Romney wins 2.2% more of the popular vote in every state in 2012 and President Obama wins 2.2% less (and Romney therefore wins the nation's popular vote by a half a percentage point), Romney still would have *lost* the electoral vote to Obama under our present winner-take-all system, 272 to 266. Under the Winner-Takes-Most system, however, Romney would have won the electoral vote as well as the popular vote, 245 to 242.

In 2008, the actual electoral vote was Obama 365, McCain 173. Under the Winner-Takes-Most system, it would have been Obama 268, McCain 219, a more equitable result considering that McCain did win 46% of the popular vote.

In 2004, instead of the actual electoral vote, Bush 286, Kerry 252, the margin under the Winner-Takes-Most reform would have been narrower, Bush 255, Kerry 232, a better reflection of the close popular vote that year.

In 2000, even with George W. Bush *winning* Florida, the electoral vote—instead of the actual result, Bush 271, Gore 266—would have been, under the Winner-Takes-Most system, Gore 245, Bush 242, again a much more accurate mirror of the nation's vote that year, considering that Gore won 48.4% of the popular vote to Bush's 47.9%.

The Winner-Takes-Most reform, because it would have allowed both Al Gore to win in 2000 and Mitt Romney to win in 2012 (if he had won an extra 2.2% of the popular vote at President Obama's expense), passes the key test of political neutrality.*

---

* The Winner-Takes-Most reform would also have worked well if George W. Bush had won ³⁄₁₀ of 1% more of the popular vote in every state in 2000 at Al Gore's expense and won the nation's popular vote, 48.2% to 48.1%. Bush would then have picked up four states—Wisconsin, Iowa, New Mexico, and Oregon—and under the Winner-Takes-Most system, the electoral vote would have been Bush 252, Gore 235.

What about elections further in the past? In 1876 Samuel Tilden won 50.9% of the nation's popular vote, but lost the election to Rutherford B. Hayes even though Hayes received only 47.9% of the vote, because after weeks of hearings, a congressional commission declared the final electoral vote to be Hayes 185, Tilden 184. But under the Winner-Takes-Most reform, even if the disputed states of Florida, Louisiana, and South Carolina had each continued to go for Hayes, Tilden would still have won the electoral vote, 169 to 162, an outcome that would have affirmed Tilden's popular-vote majority.

The Winner-Takes-Most system greatly reduces the chances of a runner-up presidency, but does not get rid of the possibility altogether. In 1888, although Benjamin Harrison lost the popular vote to Grover Cleveland, 48.6% to 47.8%, he won the electoral vote handily, 233 to 168. Under Winner-Takes-Most reform, however, the margin of Harrison's victory would have shrunk dramatically, from 65 electoral votes to just 5, although Harrison would still have edged past Cleveland: 184 electoral votes to 179.

For some, the fact that a runner-up presidency could still happen even after an innovative reform takes effect will be a reason not to reform the system at all. But the question posed earlier needs to be asked again: Why should the perfect be the enemy of the good? The Winner-Takes-Most system can make another runner-up presidency much less likely to happen without any change in the urban-rural balance of power. This is a great benefit with no cost.

Can third-party candidates win some more electoral votes under the Winner-Takes-Most system by finishing second in a state's popular vote? Yes, but in practice the Winner-Takes-Most reform will not help third parties much.

In 1992, for example, Ross Perot took 19% of the nation's popular vote, but did not win a single state. He finished second only in Utah and Maine, and under the Winner-Takes-Most format, he would have received only one electoral vote, from Utah.

What if instead Perot had held on to three-quarters of the 39% support in the national polls that he briefly enjoyed in June 1992, all the way into November? And what if he had continued to lure somewhat more votes away from President Bush than he did from Governor Clinton? The popular vote that year might have been Clinton 39%, Bush 31%, and Perot 30%, and Perot would have won nine small states: seven in the West, plus Kansas and Maine.

With the Winner-Takes-Most system, even if Perot had won 30% of the popular vote, taken 9 states, and finished second in 16 more, Clinton would still have won a majority of the electoral vote; the total would have been Clinton 290, Bush 110, Perot 87. If a third-party candidate's support is spread nationally rather than concentrated regionally, the Winner-Takes-Most format will not help the candidate much even if he or she wins as much as 30% of the vote. The lesson from crunching 1992's numbers is this: The Winner-Takes-Most reform will not weaken our two-party system, because the format will continue to make it difficult for third-party candidates to win enough electoral votes to throw an election to the House of Representatives.

Another tough test of whether an electoral system is safe or not is to apply the reform to the election of 1912, when Theodore Roosevelt, the Progressive Party candidate, received 27.4% of the nation's popular vote, more than President Taft. In the four-way race that year (Socialist Eugene Debs also won 6% of the vote), Woodrow Wilson took only 41.8% of the popular vote, but finished first in 40 states and won an electoral landslide—Wilson 435, Roosevelt 88, Taft 8—a dramatic example of how electoral votes can "magnify" a candidate's popular-vote victory.

Under the Winner-Takes-Most system, however, Wilson's landslide would have shrunk a little, to Wilson 327, Roosevelt 101, Taft 55, a much better reflection of the popular vote considering that Roosevelt and Taft together did win 50.6% of the vote.

In 1968, the third-party candidacy of Alabama's governor, George Wallace, differed from Perot's run in 1992 or Theodore Roosevelt's bid in 1912, because Wallace's support was concentrated in the South. Wallace won five states and 46 electoral votes even though his percentage of the nation's popular vote, 13.5%, was less than half that of Roosevelt's.

Wallace also finished in second place in the Carolinas and Tennessee. But the nine additional electoral votes that Wallace would have picked up in these states under the Winner-Takes-Most system would have been offset by the loss of eight other electoral votes in the five states that he won. This is because Wallace would have had to *share* some of the electoral votes in the states he won with the candidates who came in second there, Richard Nixon and Hubert Humphrey. Instead of 1968's actual electoral vote—Nixon 301, Humphrey 191, Wallace 46—the vote under the Winner-Takes-Most system would have been Nixon 251, Humphrey 195, Wallace 41, a safe outcome that would have also mirrored the popular vote more closely. (To see how other recent, close, and three-party elections would have turned out under the Winner-Takes-Most system, see chart 4 in appendix C.)

WHAT ABOUT THE STATES WITH THE FEWEST PEOPLE?

Wouldn't the Winner-Takes-Most reform be a disaster for the states with the fewest people, because every state would have one less electoral vote than it had before? Actually, no. The seven least populated states (Wyoming, Vermont, North Dakota, South Dakota, Alaska, Delaware, and Montana), as well as the District of Columbia, would *benefit* from the Winner-Takes-Most system because with only two electoral votes each, they wouldn't have enough electoral votes to divide proportionally.

Not only would the first electoral vote in each of these thinly populated states go to the state's popular-vote winner, the state's second electoral vote would also go to the winner because it would be the only vote remaining. There wouldn't be any group of votes for the top two candidates to divide proportionally, only that one last vote, which after fractions are rounded to whole numbers, would go to the state's popular-vote winner. So each of the seven smallest states would continue to be winner-take-all states. *None of these states would lose any of their electoral power*, relative to the larger states, despite the loss of an electoral vote.

"Are you sure?" a Wyoming legislator might ask. "We only have three electoral votes to begin with. Why in the world should we reduce this to two?" For the answer, look at the 2012 election returns. Wyoming gave three electoral votes to Mitt Romney, but under the Winner-Takes-Most system, it would cast only two electoral votes, a reduction in clout of 33%. By contrast, California, the most populous state, awarded all 55 of its electoral votes to Barack Obama in 2012, while under the Winner-Takes-Most reform, the state's electoral vote would have been Obama 40, Romney 14. California's *margin* of electoral votes for Obama under the Winner-Takes-Most system would have fallen from 55 to just 26 (40 minus 14), for a 51% reduction in clout.

Similarly, Texas gave 38 electoral votes to Romney and none to Obama in 2012, but under the Winner-Takes-Most reform, the split would have been Romney 27, Obama 10. Texas's *margin* of electoral votes for Romney would have shrunk from 38 to 17 (27 minus 10), for a 55% reduction in clout. (Texas would have had a slightly greater decline in clout than California in 2012 because the vote in Texas that year was a little less lopsided than it was in California.)

In each case, the reduction in the margin of electoral votes—i.e., the loss of clout—in the largest states would be a little bigger than the loss of clout in the smallest states, so the smallest states have nothing to fear from the Winner-Takes-Most reform.

CHANGING HOW THE HOUSE BREAKS A DEADLOCK

No repair of our electoral system will be complete unless we also change the way that the House of Representatives decides a presidential election when no one wins a majority of the electoral vote. As things currently stand, the House will cast its ballots on a one-state-one-vote basis, with the seven members from the seven least populated states having a vote equal to that of the 195 House members from the seven most populous states. Nobody thinks this is fair, not even the most ardent supporters of our electoral system. It is a bizarre 18th-century eccentricity.

Nearly as bad, the Senate would pick the vice president separately, which could allow the president and vice president to come from different political parties—a dangerous outcome that might encourage an assassination attempt.

Several scholars have proposed that any future constitutional amendment that reforms our electoral system should also declare that if no candidate has won a majority of the electoral vote, the House and Senate would meet in a joint session and pick a president and vice president together, with each member of each house having one vote.

Not only is this an excellent idea, it would make the Senate's support for electoral reform far more likely, because most senators would much rather join the House to choose a president than to merely pick a vice president separately.

But would the smallest states ratify such an amendment? Would legislators in Vermont and Wyoming agree to end the House's antiquated one-state-one-vote arrangement that gives them so much extra power? They just might, but it would not hurt to sweeten the deal.

In any proposed amendment, a provision could state that when a joint session of the House and Senate meets to choose a president and vice president together, this joint session shall also include the nation's governors; lieutenant governors; and, from each of the nation's 50 state legislatures, the speakers of the state houses, the majority leaders of the state senates, and the majority leaders of the state houses. (Nebraska's legislature, which has only one house, could send that house's speaker, majority leader, and majority whip.)

Allowing state government leaders to participate in so momentous a decision would strengthen the principle of federalism upon which our nation is founded. It would also greatly increase the support for electoral reform in the legislatures of the least populated states, because most governors and state legislative leaders would relish the prospect of taking part in so historic a vote.

In all, 787 people would cast ballots for president and vice president: 435 representatives, 100 US senators, 50 governors, 50 lieutenant governors, 50 state-house speakers, 50 state-senate majority leaders, 50 state-house majority leaders, and 2 officials from the District of Columbia: its mayor and its normally non-voting delegate in the House of Representatives. (This would spare America the embarrassment of having Washington, DC's people excluded from such an important vote in their own city.)

Wyoming would have eight votes in this special joint session, seven more votes than its population would justify. But Wyoming and the other small states would be giving up *less than half* of their inflated power under this reform, and California would have 60 votes in such a joint session, Texas 43 votes, and New York and Florida 34 votes each.

In 1823 James Madison wrote, "The present rule of voting for President by the House of Representatives is so great a departure from the republican principle of numerical equality ... that an amendment to the Constitution on this point is justly called for." Thomas Jefferson agreed, calling the House's one-state-one-vote procedure "the most dangerous blot on our Constitution."

To have a special joint legislative session meet after an electoral dead-lock—where the House, Senate, governors, lieutenant governors, and the nation's leading state legislators would choose a president and vice president *together*—is a much fairer and more sensible procedure than the current one-state-one-vote farce.

Indeed, changing the way the House votes after an electoral deadlock is just as important as reforming the electoral system itself. If in the future there is no consensus to adopt the Winner-Takes-Most system or any other electoral reform, there should at least be a less ambitious constitutional amendment to change the way that Congress decides a deadlocked election. That more than two centuries have passed without such a reform is really quite astonishing.

Once it became law that a special joint session of Congress and state government leaders would choose the president and vice president after an electoral deadlock, the need for flesh-and-blood electors would disappear. In a separate paragraph of the same constitutional amendment, the "college" of 538 electors could come to a dignified end four or eight years later, and we could finally have an official count of the nation's electoral votes on election night instead of six weeks later.* The automatic casting of electoral votes would also get rid of "faithless electors" such as the

---

* If electoral votes were counted automatically, without any people serving as electors, the votes would no longer have to be cast in whole numbers, but could be awarded in tenths or even one-hundredths of an electoral vote. Such precision, however, would greatly lengthen the vote-counting on election night, and could easily take days, or even weeks.

Republican who voted for George Wallace rather than Richard Nixon in 1968, or the Democrat who voted for Lloyd Bentsen instead of Michael Dukakis in 1988.

More important, if no presidential candidate has won a majority of the electoral vote, then officially counting the electoral votes on election night rather than six weeks later would shift the deal-making needed to elect a president away from the obscure electors who would meet in the nation's 50 state capitals in mid-December, and move this authority instead to the much more public and transparent US Congress (or even better, to a special joint session of Congress and state government leaders), where the deal-making belongs.

The Number of Votes Each State Has in Congress If No Presidential Candidate Wins a Majority of the Electoral Vote

State	Votes at Present	Votes under an Amendment Establishing a Special Joint Session
Alabama	1	14
Alaska	1	8
Arizona	1	16
Arkansas	1	11
California	1	60
Colorado	1	14
Connecticut	1	12
Delaware	1	8
District of Columbia	0	2
Florida	1	34
Georgia	1	21
Hawaii	1	9
Idaho	1	9
Illinois	1	25
Indiana	1	16
Iowa	1	11

State	Votes at Present	Votes under an Amendment Establishing a Special Joint Session
Kansas	1	11
Kentucky	1	13
Louisiana	1	13
Maine	1	9
Maryland	1	15
Massachusetts	1	16
Michigan	1	21
Minnesota	1	15
Mississippi	1	11
Missouri	1	15
Montana	1	8
Nebraska	1	10
Nevada	1	11
New Hampshire	1	9
New Jersey	1	19
New Mexico	1	10
New York	1	34
North Carolina	1	20
North Dakota	1	8
Ohio	1	23
Oklahoma	1	12
Oregon	1	12
Pennsylvania	1	25
Rhode Island	1	9
South Carolina	1	14
South Dakota	1	8
Tennessee	1	16
Texas	1	43
Utah	1	11

State	Votes at Present	Votes under an Amendment Establishing a Special Joint Session
Vermont	1	8
Virginia	1	18
Washington	1	17
West Virginia	1	10
Wisconsin	1	15
Wyoming	1	8
Total votes	50	787

Wyoming's Share of the US Population: 1/6 of 1%
California's Share of the US Population: 12%
Wyoming's Current Share of the House's Vote for President: 2%
California's Current Share of the House's Vote for President: 2%
Wyoming's Share of the Special Joint Session: 1.02%
California's Share of the Special Joint Session: 7.62%

ELECTORAL VOTES: THE FUTURE

Under our present electoral system, we will have another runner-up president sooner than people think. Half the country will again feel cheated of an election victory by an odd set of rules created more than two centuries ago. But if we abandon electoral votes for direct elections, there will soon be many small and extreme political parties, merging together and breaking apart in new and possibly dangerous coalitions.

To improve (rather than replace) our electoral system does not require any calculus, trigonometry, or even algebra. It does involve numbers, however, and most people see even simple arithmetic as a chore. As John Allen Paulos wrote in his delightful book, *Innumeracy*, many people dislike

> *any kind of mathematics, even arithmetic. The same people who can understand the subtlest emotional nuances in conversation, the most convoluted plots in literature, and the most intricate aspects of a legal case can't seem to grasp the most basic elements of a mathematical demonstration ... They're afraid. They've been intimidated by officious and sometimes sexist teachers.*

Still, a little arithmetic now can avoid four years of a runner-up presidency later. And with computers, the extra computations will take only a millisecond.

The 25th "Presidential Disability" Amendment as a Warning and a Model

Constitutional amendments rarely pass without a sense of urgency. Most have come from either a national movement or a national crisis. Yet if the passion for electoral reform seems weak today, the Constitution's 25th "Presidential Disability" Amendment is both a warning and a model. Proposed in 1965, it was ratified in 1967 after many people asked, "What if President Kennedy had survived his assassination but fallen into a long coma?" The 25th Amendment gives a majority of the cabinet and two-thirds of each house of Congress the power to remove a disabled president from office. And when the vice presidency becomes vacant, the amendment allows the president to nominate a new vice president, although a majority of the House and Senate must confirm the appointment.

In 1973, only six years after the states ratified the 25th Amendment, the amendment took effect in an entirely unforeseen way when Vice President Spiro Agnew resigned at the height of the Watergate crisis, pleading no contest to tax evasion to avoid the more serious charge of taking bribes. Now the nation lacked a vice president just when President Richard Nixon himself was in danger of being impeached.

Had the 25th Amendment not been ratified in 1967, the vice presidency would have remained vacant after Agnew resigned for another three years, until the expiration of his term on January 20, 1977. So when President Nixon resigned in 1974, his successor would not have been Gerald Ford, the Republican who Nixon and Congress had chosen to replace Agnew, but Carl Albert, the Democratic Speaker of the House.

Albert, a cheerful lush from Oklahoma, frequently admitted that he was not qualified to be president. Fortunately, he did not have to serve. In accordance with the new amendment, Congress confirmed President Nixon's appointment of Michigan Congressman Gerald Ford, the House Minority Leader, as America's new vice president only two months after Agnew resigned in disgrace in October 1973. Then, when President Nixon resigned himself the following August, Vice President Ford became the 38th president of the United States instead of Carl Albert.

How would the Watergate crisis have unfolded if the 25th Amendment had not been ratified? Would Republican party leaders have still been willing to force President Nixon to resign if his successor as president had not been the Republican vice president, Gerald Ford, but the Democratic Speaker of the House, Carl Albert? And with Albert in line to succeed him, would President Nixon have decided against resigning and taken his chances with an impeachment trial in the Senate? Would the Watergate crisis have lasted another year or two?

The sponsors of the 25th Amendment, by taking a prudent precaution in the 1960s against a serious omission in the Constitution regarding presidential disability, made the Watergate scandal much easier to resolve in the 1970s.* Today, a similar precaution could prevent another runner-up presidency.

THE SAFEST CHOICE: WINNER-TAKES-MOST

In 1983 the US Air Force ordered a study to assess the risk of launching the four new space shuttles. Closely analyzing previous rocket launches, the report's authors concluded that the odds of a space shuttle exploding during liftoff were 1 in 35. Unfortunately, NASA chose to ignore this study and instead made a politically influenced "engineering judgment" that the odds of an explosion could be reduced to 1 in 100,000. In fact, only 25 launches took place before the *Challenger* exploded.

Analyzing previous elections, history suggests that if American voters continue to be about evenly divided between the Republicans and Democrats, as they are now, the odds are considerably better than even that a presidential candidate will win an election with fewer popular votes than his or her opponent in the next 30 or 40 years. Even if one party becomes dominant, or if dominance shifts between one party and the

---

* In a similar manner, the "Y2K" safeguards that many companies took in 1999 to avoid disastrous computer glitches on January 1, 2000—including the duplication of corporate and financial records to ensure business continuity—also had an unforeseen benefit. Only a year and a half after the surprisingly uneventful turn of the millennium, the economic havoc that terrorists caused on September 11, 2001, was far smaller than it might have been because nearly every firm in Manhattan had already duplicated its financial records two years before.

other, the odds of electing another runner-up president in the next four or five decades are roughly 1 in 3, because even during periods of one-party dominance, there are still close elections.

Without some repairs, America's antiquated system of electoral votes is a rickety vehicle waiting to break down.

Americans have three choices:

1. Do nothing, and endure the inevitable strife of another runner-up presidency, with a great risk that hurried, ill-considered electoral reform will follow.
2. Roll the dice with direct elections or National Popular Vote, abandon the two-party system completely, and hope for the best.
3. Or, perhaps in the not too distant future, adopt Winner-Takes-Most, a minor repair that *preserves* our electoral system by reducing its distortions.

Utah's Senator Orrin Hatch once said that those who propose a new reform have the burden of proof "to show that their electoral scheme is better and safer than the present system." Winner-Takes-Most meets this test. By crunching the numbers to see how past elections would have turned out, we can see that the Winner-Takes-Most reform reflects the popular vote more closely than our current system does, yet avoids radical or unsafe results.

Of all the proposals to make our elections fairer, only the Winner-Takes-Most reform maintains the state-by-state character of presidential election campaigns that is so important to many of the electoral system's defenders. The reform would therefore be *much freer of unintended consequences* than other proposals for electoral change. As the charts of past elections in appendix C show in detail, the Winner-Takes-Most reform is measured, politically neutral, and *safe*.

Most Democrats know that Al Gore received more popular votes than George W. Bush in 2000. But few Republicans realize that if Mitt Romney had won even as much as 2.6% more of the popular vote at Obama's expense in every state, and thus won the popular vote across the nation by a full 1½ percentage points, President Obama would still have taken the northern swing states (except Ohio) and won a majority of the electoral votes, 272 to 266, making Obama the second runner-up president in 12 years.

Under the Winner-Takes-Most system, if Romney had won the popular vote in 2012, he would have won the electoral vote too. This is why the Winner-Takes-Most reform has a long-term chance—once its arithmetic is explained to a future generation of Americans who will be more comfortable with numbers than we are—to meet the daunting challenge of winning the support of the two-thirds of Congress and three-fourths of the state legislatures necessary to amend the Constitution. What is lacking today is any awareness by the public, the media, or our elected leaders of the *likelihood* of another runner-up presidency, or a sense of urgency about the need to avoid such an undemocratic outcome.

⁓

As the author of this work, I'm not so naive as to think that just because I've written a good book, Americans are suddenly going to drop everything and amend the Constitution. What would be wonderful, however, is if the Winner-Takes-Most reform could become the fifth alternative to the current system, along with direct elections, the District Plan, proportional representation, and National Popular Vote. Let the comparisons begin. The Winner-Takes-Most reform would have many fewer unintended consequences than the other four alternatives, yet would be much fairer than our current system.

The Founding Fathers may have been the most far-seeing people since biblical times, but they were younger than most of us realize. Nearly half of them were under 40. When they helped write the Constitution, James Madison was 36, Alexander Hamilton was 31, and a delegate from New Jersey, Jonathan Dayton (who would later cofound Dayton, Ohio), was only 26.

Being young, the Framers were nimble. After the election of 1800, when confusion over whether the electors were voting for president or vice president had turned the contest into a fiasco, and Aaron Burr, a vice presidential candidate, nearly became president instead of Thomas Jefferson, the Founders took only three years to pass and ratify a new constitutional amendment that separated the electoral votes for president and vice president. Never again would there be a tie vote between presidential and vice presidential running mates, nor would a president's opponent ever serve again as vice president. Faced with a clear and dangerous defect in the Constitution, the Framers not only corrected the problem, but did so in time for the next presidential election.

The Founding Fathers gave us an extraordinary Constitution, but they also understood the need for change, and did not intend to govern us from the grave. As Thomas Jefferson wrote in 1816:

> *Some men look at constitutions with sanctimonious reverence, and deem them like the Ark of the Covenant, too sacred to be touched. They ascribe to the men of the preceding age a wisdom more than human, and suppose that what they did to be beyond amendment. I knew that age well; I belonged to it . . .*
>
> *But I know also, that laws and institutions must go hand in hand with the progress of the human mind. As that becomes more developed, more enlightened, as new discoveries are made, new truths disclosed, and manners and opinions change with the change of circumstances, institutions must advance also, and keep pace with the times.*

Today, if James Madison, the creator of electoral votes, were to pay us a visit, would he really say, "My work is sacred, don't touch it"? Or might he nod and say instead, "Yes, if a little more arithmetic can make my system safer, then of course, proceed."

Appendix A

Three Possible Constitutional Amendments

Proposal 1: Direct Elections, with a Runoff If No One Wins More Than 50% of the Popular Vote

Proposal 2: Winner-Takes-Most, and Changing the Way the House Decides a Deadlocked Election

Proposal 3: Only Changing the Way the House Decides a Deadlocked Election

Proposal 1: Direct Elections, with a Runoff If No One Wins More Than 50% of the Popular Vote

AMENDMENT XXVIII

Section 1

Beginning one year after the January 21st that follows the ratification of this amendment, men and women shall no longer be elected president or vice president by accumulating electoral votes. Instead, any candidate for president or vice president who wins a majority of the nation's popular vote in a presidential election shall win that election and be inaugurated president or vice president at the beginning of the new presidential or vice presidential term.

But if no candidate for president or vice president has won more than fifty percent (50%) of the popular vote, there shall be a nationwide runoff election two weeks after the original presidential election, or on the second Tuesday in December if there has first been a national recount. The runoff election shall be between the two pairs of candidates for president and vice president who received the most popular votes nationally, and the winners of this runoff shall be inaugurated president and vice president at the beginning of the new presidential and vice presidential terms.

Section 2

A nationwide recount shall begin after a presidential election or national runoff if within four days after the last polling place has closed, the vote count at the time shows that the popular votes won by the second-place pair of presidential and vice presidential candidates is within three-tenths of one percent (³⁄₁₀ of 1%) of the total popular votes won by the pair of presidential and vice presidential candidates who appear to have won the most popular votes. A recount of a presidential election must be completed by 12:00 noon Eastern Standard Time on December 1, and a recount of a national runoff must be completed the following month by 12:00 noon Eastern Standard Time on January 5.

Section 3

Congress shall create a national, professional, and *nonpartisan* agency to oversee and administer presidential elections, recounts, and runoffs in an accurate and timely manner, and Congress shall have the power to enforce this Amendment and this section with appropriate legislation.

Section 4

This article shall be inoperative unless it shall have been ratified to the Constitution by the legislatures of three-fourths of the several states within fourteen years from the date of its submission to the states by Congress.

PROPOSAL 2: WINNER-TAKES-MOST, AND CHANGING THE WAY THE HOUSE DECIDES A DEADLOCKED ELECTION

AMENDMENT XXVIII

Section 1

Beginning one year after the January 21st that follows the ratification of this amendment, a state (or the District of Columbia) shall cast its electoral votes for president and vice president without the aid of individual electors or colleges of electors. A state's electoral votes for president and vice president shall be counted on election night, or if a recount of a state's popular vote is necessary, in time for the convening of the new US Congress.

After the votes of a state (or the District of Columbia) have been counted, the governor of that state (or in the District of Columbia, the mayor) shall promptly determine and certify the number of electoral votes earned by each candidate for president, and the number of electoral votes earned by each candidate for vice president, and then sign, seal, and transmit this certificate to the President of the US Senate.

If for any reason a state's government sends competing certificates of electoral votes to the President of the US Senate, Congress shall decide which certificate to accept in accordance with any statutes that have been signed into law at least one year before the election in question, or if the statutes are not reasonably clear, then by any other means that Congress may direct.

Section 2

The number of electoral votes that each state shall cast for president, and the number of electoral votes that each state shall cast for vice president, shall be equal to the whole number of representatives to which the state may be entitled in the House of Representatives, plus one.

The number of electoral votes for president and vice president to which the District of Columbia may be entitled shall be equal to that of the least populous state, but Congress may, by a three-fifths vote in each house, grant the District an additional electoral vote, or two, in the future if a growing population there should warrant such a change. Once granted, the extra electoral vote or votes shall not be taken away from the District of Columbia unless the removal is warranted by a population loss, in which case the loss of an electoral vote or votes following a census (or the regaining of a previously lost electoral vote following a census) shall be automatic and shall not require a congressional vote.

Section 3

The maximum number of electoral votes that a state (or the District of Columbia) may award to a presidential or vice presidential candidate on a winner-take-all basis shall be only one-third of the state's total number of electoral votes, rounded to the nearest whole number, with a minimum of one electoral vote.

The remainder of the state's (or the District of Columbia's) electoral votes for president shall be divided proportionally (but rounded up or down to whole numbers) between the two presidential candidates who have won the most popular votes within this state (or within the District of Columbia) in accordance with the number of popular votes they have won in the state or district.

The remainder of the state's (or the District of Columbia's) electoral votes for vice president shall also be divided proportionally (but rounded up or down to whole numbers) between the two vice presidential candidates who have won the most popular votes within the state (or within the District of Columbia) in accordance with the number of popular votes they have won in the state or district.

Political parties offering slates of electors shall *rank* their electors, so that the state's voters shall know which members of a party's slate shall serve as electors, and which shall not serve, should the party's presidential and vice presidential candidates win some of the state's electoral votes and not others.

Notwithstanding the previous paragraphs, the states of Maine and Nebraska shall each be free, if either one chooses, to continue its system of awarding single electoral votes for president and vice president to any presidential or vice presidential candidate who has won the most popular votes in a congressional district, and each state's one additional electoral vote shall be awarded to the presidential candidate, and vice presidential candidate, who has won the most popular votes in the state as a whole.

Section 4

If following a presidential election no presidential or vice presidential candidate has won a majority of the electoral vote (as counted within four days after the last polling place has closed after a presidential election, or if there has subsequently been a recount in one or more states, as counted by 12:00 noon Eastern Standard Time on December 3), then the term of the outgoing US Senate and the term of the outgoing House of

Representatives shall end three weeks early, and the terms of the incoming Senate and the incoming House of Representatives shall begin three weeks early, at noon Eastern Standard Time on the 13th day of December, or if such day be a Sunday, at noon on the 14th day of December.

If there is still no presidential or vice presidential candidate who has won a majority of the electoral vote by the time the incoming Senate and the incoming House of Representatives have begun their new sessions, and if this lack of an electoral majority has no reasonable chance (as determined by two of the following three officials: the President of the outgoing Senate, the Speaker of the incoming House, and the Chief Justice of the Supreme Court) of being remedied within seven days by an ongoing recount, then on the morning of December 17, or as soon as possible thereafter, a Special Joint Session of the nation's highest elected officials shall convene to choose both a president and a vice president.

Each member of this Special Joint Session shall have one equal vote. The President of the outgoing US Senate shall preside over this session, but he or she shall not have a vote (unless he or she is also a member of the incoming Congress, or is an incoming governor of a state or mayor of the District of Columbia, or is otherwise eligible to have a vote in this Session).

This Special Joint Session shall include not only each member of the Senate and the House of Representatives, it shall also include the governors and lieutenant governors of the states, the mayor of the District of Columbia, the District of Columbia's delegate in the House of Representatives (who in this session shall have a full vote), the majority leader of each state's senate, and the speaker and the majority leader of each state legislature's lower house. (If a state has a unicameral legislature, then it shall send its speaker, majority leader, and majority whip, or the equivalent, to the Special Joint Session.)

A majority of the Special Joint Session shall suffice as a quorum, but no candidate shall be elected president or vice president unless he or she receives a majority of all of the votes of the Special Joint Session, not just a majority of the quorum.

The Special Joint Session shall choose between the two presidential candidates (and separately, between the two vice presidential candidates) who have received the most electoral votes, but if neither of these candidates has won the most popular votes in the national election, then the members of the Special Joint Session shall also be free, if they wish, to vote for the presidential or vice presidential candidate who won the most popular votes in the national election.

Votes cast during the Special Joint Session shall be in public, not in secret.

Section 5

This article shall be inoperative unless it shall have been ratified to the Constitution by the legislatures of three-fourths of the several states within twenty-five years from the date of its submission to the states by Congress. The purpose of this lengthy ratification period is to give the nation's state legislators, and the people, ample time to assess the potential effect of this amendment on presidential elections.

PROPOSAL 3: ONLY CHANGING THE WAY THE HOUSE DECIDES A DEADLOCKED ELECTION

AMENDMENT XXVIII

Section 1

Beginning one year after the January 21st that follows the ratification of this amendment, if no presidential candidate or vice presidential candidate has won a majority of the electoral vote by the end of the third week of December after a presidential election, then the term of the outgoing Senate and the term of the outgoing House of Representatives shall end one week early, and the terms of the incoming Senate and the incoming House of Representatives shall begin one week early, on the morning of the 27th day of December, or if such day be a Sunday, on the morning of the 28th day of December.

If there is still no presidential or vice presidential candidate who has won a majority of the electoral vote by the time the incoming Senate and the incoming House of Representatives have begun their new sessions, then on the morning of December 30, or as soon as possible thereafter, a

Special Joint Session of the nation's highest elected officials shall convene to separately choose both a president and a vice president.

Each member of this Special Joint Session shall have one equal vote. The President of the outgoing US Senate shall preside over this session, but he or she shall not have a vote (unless he or she is also a member of the incoming Congress or is an incoming governor of a state or mayor of the District of Columbia, or is otherwise eligible to have a vote in this Session).

This Special Joint Session shall include not only each member of the Senate and the House of Representatives, it shall also include the governors and lieutenant governors of the states, the mayor of the District of Columbia, the District of Columbia's delegate in the House of Representatives (who in this session shall have a full vote), the majority leader of each state's senate, and the speaker and the majority leader of each state legislature's lower house. (If a state has a unicameral legislature, then it shall send its speaker, majority leader, and majority whip, or the equivalent, to the Special Joint Session.)

A majority of the Special Joint Session shall suffice as a quorum, but no candidate shall be elected president or vice president unless he or she receives a majority of all the votes of the Special Joint Session, not just a majority of the quorum.

The Special Joint Session shall choose between the two presidential candidates (and separately, between the two vice presidential candidates) who have received the most electoral votes, but if neither of these candidates has won the most popular votes in the national election, then the members of the Special Joint Session shall also be free, if they wish, to vote for the presidential or vice presidential candidate who won the most popular votes in the national election.

Votes cast during the Special Joint Session shall be in public, not in secret.

Section 2
Beginning four years after the January 21st that follows the ratification of this Amendment, a state (or the District of Columbia) shall cast its electoral votes for president and vice president without the aid of individual

electors or colleges of electors. A state's electoral votes for president and vice president shall simply be counted on election night, or as soon as possible thereafter.

Section 3

This article shall be inoperative unless it shall have been ratified to the Constitution by the legislatures of three-fourths of the several states within fourteen years from the date of its submission to the states by Congress.

Appendix B

Winner-Takes-Most's Roughly Equal Sacrifices from State to State

No reform of America's electoral system will ever become law unless some of the nation's 10 or 12 swing states agree to the change. For better or worse, the Winner-Takes-Most system, unlike other proposed reforms, *preserves* the power of the swing states, because even one-third-sized blocs of electoral votes will still be crucial to victory.

How do we know this? Look at Nevada. In 2012 the presidential candidates broadcast more than 80,000 television commercials in the sparsely populated state, and during the last two months of the campaign, Barack Obama, Joe Biden, Mitt Romney, and Paul Ryan together made 13 campaign trips to Nevada, more campaign stops (i.e., excluding fundraisers) than to California, Texas, New York, and Pennsylvania combined. Why? Because even Nevada's small sum of 6 electoral votes was still important.

Similarly, in 2000, George W. Bush and Al Gore broadcast almost 15,000 television commercials in the rural state of West Virginia and made dozens of campaign visits to thinly populated New Mexico, because they believed that even West Virginia's 5 electoral votes and New Mexico's 5 electoral votes were crucial to victory.

Under the Winner-Takes-Most reform, 20 states would still have vital blocs of 4 or more electoral votes at stake in a presidential election (4 electoral votes being nearly as good in a 487-electoral-vote system as 5 votes are in a 538-electoral-vote system):

Electoral Vote Blocs at Stake under the Winner-Takes-Most System

West	Midwest	South	Northeast
California (18)	Illinois (7)	Texas (12 or 13)	New York (9 or 10)
Washington (5)	Ohio (7)	Florida (9 or 10)	Pennsylvania (7)
Arizona (4)	Michigan (5)	North Carolina (6)	New Jersey (5)
Colorado* (4)	Indiana (4)	Georgia (5)	Massachusetts (4)
		Virginia (4)	
		Tennessee(4)	
		Alabama* (4)	
		South Carolina* (4)	

* Alabama, Colorado, and South Carolina, although less populous than the other states on this list, are here because of an arithmetical oddity. They are the only states with 9 electoral votes, and under the Winner-Takes-Most system, they would have just 8. In each state, 3 electoral votes would be awarded to the winner of that state's popular vote, while the remaining 5 votes would be divided proportionally between the state's top two popular-vote winners, nearly always as a split of 3 votes to 2. In practice, the fifth proportional vote would also go to the state's popular-vote winner, so there would be a bloc of 4 electoral votes at stake instead of 3. Many other states would also often have their last proportional vote be up for grabs.

None of these 20 states would lose any of their power, relative to the other states, under the Winner-Takes-Most system.

Another 12 states would each have 3 electoral votes at stake:

West	Midwest	South	Northeast
Nevada (3)	Iowa (3)	Arkansas (3)	Maryland (3)
Utah (3)	Kansas (3)	Kentucky (3)	
	Minnesota (3)	Louisiana (3)	
	Missouri (3)	Mississippi (3)	
	Wisconsin (3)		

It may seem strange that middle-sized states such as Missouri, Wisconsin, and Minnesota, each currently having 10 electoral votes, should have to give up 70% of their electoral power (because under the

Winner-Takes-Most system, only 3 of their 9 electoral votes would be at stake before the rest of their electoral votes were divided proportionally). And that the smaller states of Connecticut, Oklahoma, and Oregon, each currently having 7 electoral votes, would also have to give up 71% of their electoral power (because under the Winner-Takes-Most reform, only 2 of their 6 electoral votes would be at stake before the rest of the state's votes were divided proportionally).

But these seven states would not be the only ones sacrificing most of their electoral power. In California, for example, the number of electoral votes at stake would fall from 55 to 18, a 67% drop, while those in Texas would shrink from 38 to 12, a 68% drop. The number of electoral votes at stake in New York and Florida would also each drop from 29 to 9, another 69% decline. In fact, under the Winner-Takes-Most system, almost every state gives up about two-thirds of the electoral votes that it formerly had at stake, because the winner of a state's popular vote would take only one-third of the state's electoral votes to begin with before the rest of the state's votes were divided proportionally. So relative to the other states, Missouri, Wisconsin, and Oklahoma would not give up an unfair share of their electoral clout.

FIVE STATES SACRIFICE THE MOST—OR IS IT JUST TWO?

Five states lose the most clout under the Winner-Takes-Most system: Maine, New Hampshire, Rhode Island, Idaho, and Hawaii. Under our current system, they each have 4 electoral votes, but under the Winner-Takes-Most reform, they would have only 3. In each state, the popular-vote winner would take 1 of these 3 electoral votes to start with, while the other 2 votes would be divided proportionally. In practice, unless one presidential candidate wins nearly 75% of a state's vote, the 2 remaining electoral votes would be split evenly, 1 to 1, so the state's final electoral vote would be 2 electoral votes for one candidate and 1 electoral vote for the other. Because both candidates would win at least 1 electoral vote no matter what, the only electoral vote that would be at stake in these five states would be the first electoral vote that goes to the winner of the state's popular vote.

In each of these five states, the bloc of electoral votes at stake in a presidential election would fall from the present 4 to just 1. Although this 75% decline in votes at stake is not that much steeper than the drops of votes at stake in other states (California's votes at stake would drop 67%, and Texas's would fall 68%), it is still quite a sacrifice for a state to have only one electoral vote in contention.*

Maine, of course, has used the District Plan since 1969, so in practice Maine would continue to be a winner-take-all state. This is because its two congressional districts have nearly always voted for the same candidate in presidential elections, so the candidate winning the state would not have to split any of the state's electoral votes with his or her opponent. As a result, Maine would not suffer any sacrifice in clout under the Winner-Takes-Most system.

Legislators in Hawaii and Rhode Island should also look at the Winner-Takes-Most reform favorably. Why? Because Hawaii and Rhode Island have both already ratified National Popular Vote, a system that would often require a state to cast its electoral votes for a candidate whom a majority of the state's voters have *opposed*. In other words, the legislatures of Hawaii and Rhode Island have decided that it is more important for the nation's popular-vote winner to win the nation's electoral vote too than it is for a single state to cast its electoral votes for the particular state's popular-vote winner.

In effect, the legislators in Hawaii and Rhode Island have agreed to occasionally reduce the number of electoral votes in their states from plus 4 to *minus 4*, because this is what awarding electoral votes to someone whom most of the state's citizens have voted against amounts to. Legislators in Hawaii and Rhode Island (and in Maine, the state senators), having already ratified National Popular Vote, ought to be willing to adopt the far less sweeping Winner-Takes-Most reform as well.

---

* One possible solution to such a drastic decline in votes at stake is to agree that any constitutional amendment that enacts the Winner-Takes-Most reform could also permit states with 3 electoral votes (no more than 3, no less than 3, and *only* so long as the state has just 3 electoral votes) to adopt the District Plan (described in chapter 8). Each of these states could then award 2 of their electoral votes to the popular-vote winners in each of their two congressional districts, while the third (statewide) electoral vote would go to the winner of the state's popular vote. In practice, this would turn each of these states into winner-take-all states with 3 electoral votes each.

This leaves only two states with a reason to be wary of the Winner-Takes-Most reform: Idaho and New Hampshire. Idaho (although it might be willing to follow Maine and adopt the District Plan) rarely supports reforms of any kind. And New Hampshire's role in presidential nominations is so grossly exaggerated that it would be hard to feel sorry for the state if its clout during a general election dropped 75%, especially if the clout in nearby Connecticut fell 71%, and in New York 69%. New Hampshire would also continue to be a swing state under the Winner-Takes-Most reform. Even with just one electoral vote left at stake, New Hampshire would still be better off than the 39 "spectator" states that currently have no electoral votes in contention. And unlike other reforms, the Winner-Takes-Most format *preserves* the role of the swing states, which is to New Hampshire's advantage.

Appendix C

Past Elections under the Winner-Takes-Most Reform

Chart 1: 2012

Chart 2: 2012 (If Romney Had Won 2.2% More of the Popular Vote)

Chart 3: 2000

Chart 4: Recent, Close, Three-Party and Four-Party Elections (1860–2012)

Chart 1

Electoral Votes in 2012 under the Winner-Take-All and Winner-Takes-Most Systems

(States for Romney are shaded.)

State	Popular Vote % Obama / Romney	Winner-Take-All Obama / Romney	Winner-Takes-Most Obama / Romney
Alabama	O 38 / R 61	Obama 0, Romney 9	Obama 2, Romney 6
Alaska	O 41 / R 55	Obama 0, Romney 3	Obama 0, Romney 2
Arizona	O 44 / R 53	Obama 0, Romney 11	Obama 3, Romney 7
Arkansas	O 37 / R 61	Obama 0, Romney 6	Obama 1, Romney 4
California	O 60 / R 37	Obama 55, Romney 0	Obama 40, Romney 14
Colorado	O 51 / R 46	Obama 9, Romney 0	Obama 6, Romney 2
Connecticut	O 58 / R 41	Obama 7, Romney 0	Obama 4, Romney 2
Delaware	O 59 / R 40	Obama 3, Romney 0	Obama 2, Romney 0
District of Columbia	O 91 / R 7	Obama 3, Romney 0	Obama 2, Romney 0
Florida	O 50 / R 49	Obama 29, Romney 0	Obama 19, Romney 9
Georgia	O 45 / R 53	Obama 0, Romney 16	Obama 5, Romney 10
Hawaii	O 71 / R 28	Obama 4, Romney 0	Obama 2, Romney 1
Idaho	O 32 / R 64	Obama 0, Romney 4	Obama 1, Romney 2
Illinois	O 58 / R 41	Obama 20, Romney 0	Obama 13, Romney 6
Indiana	O 44 / R 54	Obama 0, Romney 11	Obama 3, Romney 7
Iowa	O 52 / R 46	Obama 6, Romney 0	Obama 4, Romney 1
Kansas	O 38 / R 60	Obama 0, Romney 6	Obama 1, Romney 4
Kentucky	O 38 / R 60	Obama 0, Romney 8	Obama 2, Romney 5

State	Popular Vote		
Louisiana	O 41 / R 58	Obama 0, Romney 8	Obama 2, Romney 5
Maine	O 56 / R 41	Obama 4, Romney 0	Obama 3, Romney 0*
Maryland	O 62 / R 36	Obama 10, Romney 0	Obama 7, Romney 2
Massachusetts	O 61 / R 38	Obama 11, Romney 0	Obama 7, Romney 3
Michigan	O 54 / R 45	Obama 16, Romney 0	Obama 10, Romney 5
Minnesota	O 53 / R 45	Obama 10, Romney 0	Obama 6, Romney 3
Mississippi	O 44 / R 55	Obama 0, Romney 6	Obama 1, Romney 4
Missouri	O 44 / R 54	Obama 0, Romney 10	Obama 2, Romney 7
Montana	O 42 / R 55	Obama 0, Romney 3	Obama 0, Romney 2
Nebraska	O 38 / R 60	Obama 0, Romney 5	Obama 0, Romney 4*
Nevada	O 52 / R 46	Obama 6, Romney 0	Obama 4, Romney 1
New Hampshire	O 52 / R 46	Obama 4, Romney 0	Obama 2, Romney 1
New Jersey	O 58 / R 41	Obama 14, Romney 0	Obama 9, Romney 4
New Mexico	O 53 / R 43	Obama 5, Romney 0	Obama 3, Romney 1
New York	O 63 / R 35	Obama 29, Romney 0	Obama 21, Romney 7
North Carolina	O 48 / R 50	Obama 0, Romney 15	Obama 4, Romney 10
North Dakota	O 39 / R 58	Obama 0, Romney 3	Obama 0, Romney 2
Ohio	O 51 / R 48	Obama 18, Romney 0	Obama 12, Romney 5
Oklahoma	O 33 / R 67	Obama 0, Romney 7	Obama 1, Romney 5
Oregon	O 54 / R 42	Obama 7, Romney 0	Obama 4, Romney 2
Pennsylvania	O 52 / R 47	Obama 20, Romney 0	Obama 13, Romney 6
Rhode Island	O 63 / R 35	Obama 4, Romney 0	Obama 2, Romney 1
South Carolina	O 44 / R 55	Obama 0, Romney 9	Obama 2, Romney 6

State	Popular Vote % Obama / Romney	Winner-Take-All Obama / Romney	Winner-Takes-Most Obama / Romney
South Dakota	O 45 / R 58	Obama 0, Romney 3	Obama 0, Romney 2
Tennessee	O 42 / R 59	Obama 0, Romney 11	Obama 3, Romney 7
Texas	O 41 / R 57	Obama 0, Romney 38	Obama 10, Romney 27
Utah	O 25 / R 73	Obama 0, Romney 6	Obama 1, Romney 4
Vermont	O 67 / R 31	Obama 3, Romney 0	Obama 2, Romney 0
Virginia	O 51 / R 47	Obama 13, Romney 0	Obama 8, Romney 4
Washington	O 56 / R 41	Obama 12, Romney 0	Obama 8, Romney 3
West Virginia	O 36 / R 62	Obama 0, Romney 5	Obama 1, Romney 3
Wisconsin	O 53 / R 46	Obama 10, Romney 0	Obama 6, Romney 3
Wyoming	O 28 / R 69	Obama 0, Romney 3	Obama 0, Romney 2
2012 Totals	**O 51.01 / R 47.15**	**Obama 332, Romney 206**	**Obama 264, Romney 223**

* Maine (since 1969) and Nebraska (since 1992) award electoral votes by congressional district rather than by winner-take-all and have 2 additional statewide electoral votes under the current system, but only 1 additional statewide electoral vote under the Winner-Takes-Most system. Under the Winner-Takes-Most reform, however, if most of Maine's and Nebraska's electoral votes are awarded by congressional district, then the two states will each only have 1 vote left to divide proportionally, and after totals are rounded to whole numbers, the state's popular-vote winner will take that last electoral vote too.

Under the Winner-Takes-Most system, each state has one less electoral vote than before, and the winner of a state's popular vote takes only one-third of the state's electoral votes (rounding to the nearest whole number above zero) to start with. The rest of the state's electoral votes are divided proportionally (but rounded to whole numbers) between the state's top two (and only the top two) popular-vote winners, in proportion to the popular votes they won in the state.

With 51 fewer electoral votes than before, the total number of electoral votes under the Winner-Takes-Most system is 487; 244 are required to win the presidency.

Chart 2

Electoral Votes in 2012 under the Winner-Take-All and Winner-Takes-Most Systems If Romney Had Won 2.2% More of the Popular Vote in Every State (and Obama Had Won 2.2% Less)

(States for Romney are shaded.)

State	Popular Vote % Obama / Romney	Winner-Take-All Obama / Romney	Winner-Takes-Most Obama / Romney
Alabama	O 36.2 / R 62.8	Obama 0, Romney 9	Obama 2, Romney 6
Alaska	O 38.6 / R 57.0	Obama 0, Romney 3	Obama 0, Romney 2
Arizona	O 42.3 / R 55.7	Obama 0, Romney 11	Obama 3, Romney 7
Arkansas	O 34.7 / R 62.8	Obama 0, Romney 6	Obama 1, Romney 4
California	O 58.0 / R 39.3	Obama 55, Romney 0	Obama 39, Romney 15
Colorado	O 49.3 / R 48.3	Obama 9, Romney 0	Obama 6, Romney 2
Connecticut	O 55.9 / R 42.9	Obama 7, Romney 0	Obama 4, Romney 2
Delaware	O 56.4 / R 42.2	Obama 3, Romney 0	Obama 2, Romney 0
District of Columbia	O 88.7 / R 9.5	Obama 3, Romney 0	Obama 2, Romney 0
Florida	O 47.7 / R 51.2	Obama 0, Romney 29	Obama 9, Romney 19
Georgia	O 43.3 / R 55.5	Obama 0, Romney 16	Obama 4, Romney 11
Hawaii	O 68.4 / R 30.0	Obama 4, Romney 0	Obama 2, Romney 1
Idaho	O 30.2 / R 66.3	Obama 0, Romney 4	Obama 1, Romney 2
Illinois	O 55.4 / R 42.9	Obama 20, Romney 0	Obama 13, Romney 6
Indiana	O 41.7 / R 56.3	Obama 0, Romney 11	Obama 3, Romney 7
Iowa	O 49.8 / R 48.4	Obama 6, Romney 0	Obama 4, Romney 1
Kansas	O 35.8 / R 61.9	Obama 0, Romney 6	Obama 1, Romney 4

State	Popular Vote % Obama / Romney	Winner-Take-All Obama / Romney	Winner-Takes-Most Obama / Romney
Kentucky	O 35.6 / R 62.7	Obama 0, Romney 8	Obama 2, Romney 5
Louisiana	O 38.4 / R 60.0	Obama 0, Romney 8	Obama 2, Romney 5
Maine	O 54.1 / R 43.2	Obama 4, Romney 0	Obama 3, Romney 0*
Maryland	O 59.8 / R 38.1	Obama 10, Romney 0	Obama 7, Romney 2
Massachusetts	O 58.5 / R 39.7	Obama 11, Romney 0	Obama 7, Romney 3
Michigan	O 52.0 / R 46.9	Obama 16, Romney 0	Obama 10, Romney 5
Minnesota	O 50.5 / R 47.2	Obama 10, Romney 0	Obama 6, Romney 3
Mississippi	O 41.6 / R 57.5	Obama 0, Romney 6	Obama 1, Romney 4
Missouri	O 42.2 / R 56.0	Obama 0, Romney 10	Obama 3, Romney 6
Montana	O 39.5 / R 57.6	Obama 0, Romney 3	Obama 0, Romney 2
Nebraska	O 35.8 / 62.0	Obama 0, Romney 5	Obama 0, Romney 4*
Nevada	O 50.2 / R 47.9	Obama 6, Romney 0	Obama 4, Romney 1
New Hampshire	O 49.8 / R 48.6	Obama 4, Romney 0	Obama 2, Romney 1
New Jersey	O 56.0 / R 42.7	Obama 14, Romney 0	Obama 9, Romney 4
New Mexico	O 50.8 / R 45.0	Obama 5, Romney 0	Obama 3, Romney 1
New York	O 61.1 / R 37.4	Obama 29, Romney 0	Obama 21, Romney 7
North Carolina	O 46.2 / R 52.6	Obama 0, Romney 15	Obama 4, Romney 10
North Dakota	O 36.5 / R 60.5	Obama 0, Romney 3	Obama 0, Romney 2
Ohio	O 48.5 / R 49.9	Obama 0, Romney 18	Obama 5, Romney 12
Oklahoma	O 31.0 / R 69.0	Obama 0, Romney 7	Obama 1, Romney 5
Oregon	O 52.0 / R 44.4	Obama 7, Romney 0	Obama 4, Romney 2

Pennsylvania	O 49.8 / R 48.8	Obama 20, Romney 0	Obama 13, Romney 6
Rhode Island	O 60.5 / R 37.4	Obama 4, Romney 0	Obama 2, Romney 1
South Carolina	O 41.9 / R 56.8	Obama 0, Romney 9	Obama 2, Romney 6
South Dakota	O 37.7 / R 60.1	Obama 0, Romney 3	Obama 0, Romney 2
Tennessee	O 36.9 / R 61.7	Obama 0, Romney 11	Obama 3, Romney 7
Texas	O 39.2 / R 59.4	Obama 0, Romney 38	Obama 10, Romney 27
Utah	O 22.5 / R 74.8	Obama 0, Romney 6	Obama 1, Romney 4
Vermont	O 64.4 / R 33.2	Obama 3, Romney 0	Obama 2, Romney 0
Virginia	O 49.0 / R 49.5	Obama 0, Romney 13	Obama 4, Romney 8
Washington	O 54.0 / R 43.5	Obama 12, Romney 0	Obama 8, Romney 3
West Virginia	O 33.3 / R 64.5	Obama 0, Romney 5	Obama 1, Romney 3
Wisconsin	O 50.6 / R 48.1	Obama 10, Romney 0	Obama 6, Romney 3
Wyoming	O 25.6 / R 70.8	Obama 0, Romney 3	Obama 0, Romney 2
2012 Totals	**R 49.35 / O 48.81**	**Obama 272, Romney 266**	**Obama 242, Romney 245**

* Maine (since 1969) and Nebraska (since 1992) award electoral votes by congressional district rather than by winner-take-all and have 2 additional statewide electoral votes under the current system, but only 1 additional statewide electoral vote under the Winner-Takes-Most system. Under the Winner-Takes-Most reform, however, if most of Maine's and Nebraska's electoral votes are awarded by congressional district, then the two states will each only have 1 vote left to divide proportionally, and after totals are rounded to whole numbers, the state's popular-vote winner will take that last electoral vote too.

Under the Winner-Takes-Most system, each state has one less electoral vote than before, and the winner of a state's popular vote takes only one-third of the state's electoral votes (rounding to the nearest whole number above zero) to start with. The rest of the state's electoral votes are divided proportionally (but rounded to whole numbers) between the state's top two (and only the top two) popular-vote winners, in proportion to the popular votes they won in the state.

With 51 fewer electoral votes than before, the total number of electoral votes under the Winner-Takes-Most system is 487; 244 are required to win the presidency.

Chart 3

Electoral Votes in 2000 under the Winner-Take-All and Winner-Takes-Most Systems

(States for Bush are shaded.)

(The third number in the second column is the percentage of the popular vote for Ralph Nader, but he wins no electoral votes under either system.)

State	Popular Vote % Bush / Gore / Nader	Winner-Take-All Bush / Gore	Winner-Takes-Most Bush / Gore
Alabama	B 56 / G 42 / N 1	Bush 9, Gore 0	Bush 6, Gore 2
Alaska	B 59 / G 28 / N 10	Bush 3, Gore 0	Bush 2, Gore 0
Arizona	B 51 / G 45 / N 3	Bush 8, Gore 0	Bush 5, Gore 2
Arkansas	B 51 / G 46 / N 1	Bush 6, Gore 0	Bush 4, Gore 1
California	B 42 / G 53 / N 4	Bush 0, Gore 54	Bush 15, Gore 38
Colorado	B 51 / G 42 / N 5	Bush 8, Gore 0	Bush 5, Gore 2
Connecticut	B 38 / G 56 / N 4	Bush 0, Gore 8	Bush 2, Gore 5
Delaware	B 42 / G 55 / N 3	Bush 0, Gore 3	Bush 0, Gore 2
District of Columbia	B 9 / G 85 / N 5	Bush 0, Gore 2*	Bush 0, Gore 2
Florida	B 48.85 / G 48.84 / N 1.63	Bush 25, Gore 0	Bush 16, Gore 8
Georgia	B 55 / G 43 / N 1	Bush 13, Gore 0	Bush 8, Gore 4
Hawaii	B 37 / G 56 / N 6	Bush 0, Gore 4	Bush 1, Gore 2
Idaho	B 67 / G 28 / N 2	Bush 4, Gore 0	Bush 2, Gore 1
Illinois	B 43 / G 55 / N 2	Bush 0, Gore 22	Bush 6, Gore 15

Indiana	B 57 / G 41 / N 1	Bush 12, Gore 0	Bush 8, Gore 3
Iowa	B 48 / G 49 / N 2	Bush 0, Gore 7	Bush 2, Gore 4
Kansas	B 58 / G 37 / N 3	Bush 6, Gore 0	Bush 4, Gore 1
Kentucky	B 57 / G 41 / N 1.5	Bush 8, Gore 0	Bush 5, Gore 2
Louisiana	B 53 / G 45 / N 1	Bush 9, Gore 0	Bush 6, Gore 2
Maine	B 44 / G 49 / N 6	Bush 0, Gore 4	Bush 0, Gore 3**
Maryland	B 40 / G 57 / N 3	Bush 0, Gore 10	Bush 2, Gore 7
Massachusetts	B 33 / G 60 / N 6	Bush 0, Gore 12	Bush 2, Gore 9
Michigan	B 46 / G 51 / N 2	Bush 0, Gore 18	Bush 5, Gore 12
Minnesota	B 46 / G 48 / N 5	Bush 0, Gore 10	Bush 3, Gore 6
Mississippi	B 58 / G 41 / N 1	Bush 7, Gore 0	Bush 4, Gore 2
Missouri	B 50 / G 47 / N 2	Bush 11, Gore 0	Bush 7, Gore 3
Montana	B 58 / G 33 / N 6	Bush 3, Gore 0	Bush 2, Gore 0
Nebraska	B 62 / G 33 / N 4	Bush 5, Gore 0	Bush 4, Gore 0**
Nevada	B 50 / G 46 / N 2	Bush 4, Gore 0	Bush 2, Gore 1
New Hampshire	B 48 / G 47 / N 4	Bush 4, Gore 0	Bush 2, Gore 1
New Jersey	B 40 / G 56 / N 3	Bush 0, Gore 15	Bush 4, Gore 10
New Mexico	B 47.85 / G 47.91 / N 4	Bush 0, Gore 5	Bush 1, Gore 3
New York	B 35 / G 60 / N 4	Bush 0, Gore 33	Bush 8, Gore 24

State	Popular Vote % Bush / Gore / Nader	Winner-Take-All Bush / Gore	Winner-Takes-Most Bush / Gore
North Carolina	B 56 / G 43 / N 0***	Bush 14, Gore 0	Bush 9, Gore 4
North Dakota	B 61 / G 33 / N 3	Bush 3, Gore 0	Bush 2, Gore 0
Ohio	B 50 / G 46 / N 2.5	Bush 21, Gore 0	Bush 14, Gore 6
Oklahoma	B 60 / G 38 / N 0***	Bush 8, Gore 0	Bush 5, Gore 2
Oregon	B 46.5 / G 47 / N 5	Bush 0, Gore 7	Bush 2, Gore 4
Pennsylvania	B 46 / G 51 / N 2	Bush 0, Gore 23	Bush 7, Gore 15
Rhode Island	B 32 / G 61 / N 6	Bush 0, Gore 4	Bush 1, Gore 2
South Carolina	B 57 / G 41 / N 1*	Bush 8, Gore 0	Bush 5, Gore 2
South Dakota	B 60 / G 38 / N 0***	Bush 3, Gore 0	Bush 2, Gore 0
Tennessee	B 51 / G 47 / N 1	Bush 11, Gore 0	Bush 7, Gore 3
Texas	B 59 / G 38 / N 2	Bush 32, Gore 0	Bush 23, Gore 8
Utah	B 67 / G 26 / N 5	Bush 5, Gore 0	Bush 3, Gore 1
Vermont	B 41 / G 51 / N 7	Bush 0, Gore 3	Bush 0, Gore 2
Virginia	B 52 / G 44 / N 2	Bush 13, Gore 0	Bush 8, Gore 4
Washington	B 45 / G 50 / N 4	Bush 0, Gore 11	Bush 3, Gore 7
West Virginia	B 52 / G 46 / N 2	Bush 5, Gore 0	Bush 3, Gore 1
Wisconsin	B 47.6 / G 47.8 / N 4	Bush 0, Gore 11	Bush 3, Gore 7

State	Popular Vote % Bush / Gore / Nader	Winner-Take-All Bush / Gore	Winner-Takes-Most Bush / Gore
Wyoming	B 68 / G 28 / N 2	Bush 3, Gore 0	Bush 2, Gore 0
2000 Totals	**G 48.4 / B 47.9 / N 2.7**	**Bush 271, Gore 266, Nader 0**	**Bush 242, Gore 245, Nader 0**

* In 2000 one of the three electors pledged to Al Gore from the District of Columbia left her ballot blank to protest the District of Columbia's lack of representation in Congress. The total electoral vote that year was therefore Bush 271, Gore 266, instead of Bush 271, Gore 267.

** Maine (since 1969) and Nebraska (since 1992) have awarded electoral votes by congressional district rather than by winner-take-all and have 2 additional statewide electoral votes under the present system, but only 1 additional statewide electoral vote under the Winner-Takes-Most system. Under the Winner-Takes-Most reform, however, if most of Maine's and Nebraska's electoral votes are awarded by congressional district, then the two states will each only have 1 vote left to divide proportionally, and after totals are rounded to whole numbers, the state's popular-vote winner will take that last electoral vote too.

*** Nader was not on the ballot in North Carolina, Oklahoma, or South Dakota in 2000.

Under the Winner-Takes-Most system, each state has one less electoral vote than before, and the winner of a state's popular vote takes only one-third of the state's electoral votes (rounding to the nearest whole number above zero) to start with. The rest of the state's electoral votes are divided proportionally (but rounded to whole numbers) between the state's top two (and only the top two) popular-vote winners, in proportion to the popular votes they won in the state.

With 51 fewer electoral votes than before, the total number of electoral votes under the Winner-Takes-Most system is 487; 244 are required to win the presidency.

Chart 4

Past Elections: Recent, Close, Three-Party and Four-Party Presidential Elections under the Winner-Takes-Most Reform*

(The winner's numbers are in **boldface**. The elections of 1876 and 2000 and the hypothetical election of 2012 (where Romney receives an extra 2.2% of the vote at Obama's expense) are in *italics* because the Winner-Takes-Most system would have changed the outcome.

Democratic Party = shaded
Republican Party = unshaded
All third parties = unshaded with gray text

Year	Candidates	Popular Vote	Actual Electoral Vote	Under Winner-Takes-Most
2012 (Actual)	**Obama**	**51.06%**	**332**	**264**
	Romney	47.21%	206	223
2012 (Hypothetical, see chapter 10)	*Romney*	*49.41%*	*266*	*245*
	Obama	*48.86%*	*272*	*242*
2008	**Obama**	**52.9%**	**365**	**268**
	McCain	45.6%	173	219
2004	**G. W. Bush**	**50.7%**	**286**	**255**
	Kerry	48.3%	252	232
2000	*G. W. Bush*	*47.9%*	*271*	*242*
	Gore	*48.4%*	*266*	*245*
	Nader	*2.7%*	*0*	*0*
1996	**Clinton**	**49.2%**	**379**	**290**
	Dole	40.7%	159	197
	Perot	8.4%	0	0
1992	**Clinton**	**43.0%**	**370**	**282**
	G. H. W. Bush	37.5%	168	204
	Perot	18.9%	0	1
1988	**G. H. W. Bush**	**53.4%**	**426**	**308**
	Dukakis	45.7%	111	179

1984	Reagan	58.8%	525	351
	Mondale	40.6%	13	136
1980	Reagan	50.8%	489	332
	Carter	41.0%	49	155
	Anderson	6.6%	0	0
1976	Carter	50.1%	297	249
	Ford	48.0%	240	238
	McCarthy	0.9%	0	0
1968	Nixon	43.4%	301	251
	Humphrey	42.7%	191	195
	G. Wallace	13.5%	46	41
1960**	Kennedy	49.7%	303	260
	Nixon	49.6%	219	222
	Byrd	0.7%	15	5
1948***	Truman	49.6%	303	256
	Dewey	45.1%	189	195
	Thurmond	2.4%	39	32
	H. Wallace	2.4%	0	0
1924	Coolidge	54.0%	382	296
	Davis	28.8%	136	162
	La Follette	16.6%	13	25
1916	Wilson	49.2%	277	263
	Hughes	46.1%	254	219
	Benson	3.2%	0	0
	Hanly	1.2%	0	1
1912	Wilson	41.8%	435	327
	T. Roosevelt	27.4%	88	101
	Taft	23.2%	8	55
	Debs	6.0%	0	0
1892	Cleveland	46.0%	277	218
	B. Harrison	43.0%	145	157
	Weaver	8.5%	22	25

1888	**B. Harrison**	**47.8%**	**233**	**184**
	Cleveland	48.6%	168	179
	Fisk	2.2%	0	0
1884	**Cleveland**	**48.9%**	**219**	**196**
	Blaine	48.3%	182	167
	Butler	1.7%	0	0
1880	**Garfield**	**48.3%**	**214**	**171**
	Hancock	48.2%	155	160
	Weaver	3.3%	0	0
1876	*Hayes*	*47.9%*	*185*	*162*
	Tilden	*50.9%*	*184*	*169*
1860 (see the next two pages)	**Lincoln**	**39.8%**	**180**	**116**
	Breckinridge	18.1%	72	56
	Bell	12.6%	39	43
	Douglas	29.5%	12	56

* Compiled with data from the state-by-state election totals in Dave Leip's *Atlas of U.S. Presidential Elections*, http://uselectionatlas.org, last accessed November 5, 2015.

** In 1960 there were 537 electoral votes because with the addition of Alaska and Hawaii, the House of Representatives had 437 members instead of the usual 435, and the District of Columbia did not yet have 3 electoral votes. Under the Winner-Takes-Most system that year, there would have been 50 fewer electoral votes than there actually were, for a total of 487.

*** From 1912 through 1956 there were only 531 electoral votes because there were 435 members of the House of Representatives and—before the admission of Alaska and Hawaii—96 members of the Senate. Under the Winner-Takes-Most system, there would have been 48 fewer electoral votes than there actually were, for a total of 483, with 242 votes required to win the presidency.

Under the Winner-Takes-Most system, each state has one less electoral vote than before, and the winner of a state's popular vote takes only one-third of the state's electoral votes (rounding to the nearest whole number above zero) to start with. The rest of the state's electoral votes are divided proportionally (but rounded to whole numbers) between the state's top two (and only the top two) popular-vote winners, in proportion to the popular votes they won in the state.

With 51 fewer electoral votes than before, the total number of electoral votes under the Winner-Takes-Most system is 487; 244 are required to win the presidency.

In 1860, under the Winner-Takes-Most system, 136 electoral votes would have been required to win the presidency, and Lincoln would have fallen 20 votes short. While it is possible that of the 155 electors opposed to Lincoln, 136 of them might have united on a compromise candidate, a different outcome seems more likely. If no candidate had won a majority of the electoral vote by mid-December, the election would have shifted in January to the House of Representatives, as it did after the four-candidate election of 1824–25. Had this happened, the seven states of the Deep South might not have seceded so quickly if Lincoln had not yet been elected president.

If the House of Representatives of a still-united nation of 33 states had convened to elect a president early in 1861, Lincoln would have had the support of only 14 of the delegations, and the 12th Amendment would have required the House to choose a president only from the top *three* electoral-vote winners. Under the Winner-Takes-Most system, Secretary of War John Bell of Tennessee, the Constitutional Union Party candidate who took no position at all on slavery, would no longer have been eligible for the presidency because he would have won fewer electoral votes than Stephen Douglas, the neutral-on-slavery senator from Illinois, or Vice President John Breckinridge, the pro-slavery candidate from Kentucky.

Three of the Northern states had Democratic congressional majorities: New Jersey, Illinois, and Oregon. Their delegations, along with Missouri's, would almost certainly have supported Douglas, while Connecticut's delegation would have been deadlocked because it was evenly divided between Democratic and Republican representatives.

Among the Southern congressmen, the three delegations from the states that went for John Bell—Virginia, Kentucky, and Tennessee—would probably have voted for the pro-slavery candidate, John Breckinridge, because Bell was out of the running, although Douglas would have had an outside chance of winning Kentucky's delegation because he was popular with Kentucky's moderates.

On the House's first ballot for president, Lincoln might have won 14 states, Breckinridge 13 or 14 states, and Douglas 4 or 5, with Connecticut deadlocked and therefore not voting. The Southern states would then have had a major decision to make, whether to: 1) agree on Stephen

Douglas as a compromise candidate even though Douglas said that each new territory should have the right to decide for itself whether to permit slavery or not, or 2) secede from the union.

Because most Southerners had already bolted from the Democratic Party the previous spring rather than support Douglas and admit that voters in the new territories had the right to outlaw slavery, it seems likely that the seven states of the Deep South would still have seceded from the union in the winter of 1861, just as they did in real life. Then, in a smaller nation with only 26 states, Lincoln might have won the vote in what was left of the House of Representatives, with 14 states for Lincoln, 6 or 7 of the eight slave states that still remained in the union voting for Breckinridge, and 4 or 5 states supporting Douglas.

Lincoln's eventual victory under the Winner-Takes-Most system would have been far dicier and more nerve-racking than it was under the actual electoral system. But the Winner-Takes-Most system would also have given the many supporters of Stephen Douglas and John Bell—the neutral, "middle-of-the-road" voters who actually outnumbered Lincoln voters in the polarized election of 1860—a much fairer result, giving these two candidates (who together received 42% of the popular vote) 37% of the electoral vote instead of the 17% that they actually received.

The clear moral need to challenge the evil of slavery makes the 1860 election an exception, but in general if a voting system gives moderate voters more power, and strident voters (who only rarely are led by someone as great as Lincoln) less power, this is a good outcome, not a bad one.

ACKNOWLEDGMENTS

I WANT TO START BY THANKING SENATOR BILL BRADLEY, SENATOR Wyche Fowler Jr, and the *PBS NewsHour*'s longtime executive producer, Les Crystal, for their early praise and encouragement, even before this book was ready for publication.

Many people helped me with *The Runner-Up Presidency*. My agent, Peter Rubie, was knowledgeable, efficient, and, most important, patient during the long journey from manuscript to book.

I give special thanks to my editor, Keith Wallman, who spurred me to simplify the math at the end of this book. I would also like to thank senior production editor Meredith Dias, copy editor Elissa Curcio, and proofreader Kris Patenaude for their hard, rigorous work.

I am grateful to the staffs of the New York Public Library and the libraries at Dartmouth College, the University of Georgia, and in my hometown, Armonk, New York. I am also indebted to Ralph Tamlyn, a classification metadata consultant with a long career at IBM, who offered superb advice about the whole book and particularly on how best to present the many numbers in chapters 9 and 10 and in the appendices. (Any errors in this book are strictly my own.)

I'm also grateful to Professor Judith Best of the State University of New York at Cortland, and to Robert Ackerman, Donny Roberts, Arlette Jassel Goldstein, and Eric Weston, for their willingness to read an earlier draft of this book that had even more math in the final chapters than this one does. Their comments were astute and improved the book significantly.

I could not have written this book without several visits each to two quiet and supportive colonies for writers. At the Dorset Colony House in Dorset, Vermont, I give my warmest thanks to the directors, John and Paula Nassivera, for their friendship and continual encouragement. I am also indebted to the helpful and friendly staff at the Hambidge Center in Rabun Gap, Georgia.

ACKNOWLEDGMENTS

My deepest thanks go to my mother, Marybeth Weston, a writer herself who gave me excellent advice as this book progressed, and to my loving wife, artist Linda Richichi, whose spirit is as beautiful as her painting.

Selected Bibliography

BOOKS IN FAVOR OF ELECTORAL REFORM

Abbott, David W., and James P. Levine. *Wrong Winner: The Coming Debacle in the Electoral College.* New York and Westport, CT: Praeger, 1991.

Bennett, Robert W. *Taming the Electoral College.* Palo Alto, CA: Stanford University Press, 2006.

Edwards, George C., III. *Why the Electoral College Is Bad for America.* New Haven, CT: Yale University Press, 2004.

Koza, John R. *Every Vote Equal: A State-Based Plan for Electing the President by National Popular Vote.* Los Altos, CA: National Popular Vote Press, 2011.

Longley, Lawrence D., and Alan G. Braun. *The Politics of Electoral College Reform.* New Haven, CT: Yale University Press, 1972.

Longley, Lawrence D., and Neal R. Peirce. *The Electoral College Primer 2000.* New Haven, CT: Yale University Press, 1999.

Michener, James A. *Presidential Lottery: The Reckless Gamble in Our Electoral System.* New York: Random House, 1969.

Peirce, Neal R., and Lawrence D. Longley. *The People's President: The Electoral College in American History and the Direct Vote Alternative.* New Haven, CT: Yale University Press, 1981.

Schumaker, Paul D., and Burdett A. Loomis, eds. *Choosing a President: The Electoral College and Beyond.* New York and London: Chatham House Publishers/Seven Bridges Press, 2002.

BOOKS OPPOSING ELECTORAL REFORM

Berns, Walter, ed. *After the People Vote: A Guide to the Electoral College.* Washington, DC: American Enterprise Institute Press, 1992.

Best, Judith A. *The Case Against Direct Election of the President: A Defense of the Electoral College.* Ithaca, NY: Cornell University Press, 1975.

———. *The Choice of the People? Debating the Electoral College.* Lanham, MD: Rowman & Littlefield, 1996.

Bickel, Alexander M. *Reform and Continuity: The Electoral College, the Constitution, and the Party System.* New York: Harper & Row, 1971.

Glennon, Michael J. *When No Majority Rules: The Electoral College and Presidential Succession*. Washington, DC: Congressional Quarterly, 1992.

Gregg, Gary L., ed. *Securing Democracy: Why We Have an Electoral College*. Wilmington, DE: ISI Books, 2001.

Hardaway, Robert M. *The Electoral College and the Constitution: The Case for Preserving Federalism*. Westport, CT: Praeger, 1994.

Ross, Tara. *Enlightened Democracy: The Case for the Electoral College*. Dallas, TX: Colonial Press, 2004.

DATA, REPORTS, AND INFORMATIONAL BOOKS

Congressional Research Service. "The Electoral College: An Overview and Analysis of Reform Proposals," by L. Paige Whitaker and Thomas H. Neale. Washington, DC: CRS Report for Congress, updated November 5, 2004 (Order Code RL30804).

Kura, Alexandra, ed. *Electoral College and Presidential Elections*. Huntington, NY: Nova Science Publishers, 2001.

League of Women Voters. "Pros and Cons of the National Popular Vote Interstate Compact," public forum held in Norman, OK, February 12, 2009. Accessed November 5, 2015. www.norman.ok.lwvnet.org/national_popular_vote.html.

Leip, David. *David Leip's Atlas of U.S. Presidential Elections*. Accessed November 5, 2015. http://uselectionatlas.org.

Paulos, John Allen. *Innumeracy, Mathematical Illiteracy and its Consequences*. New York: Vintage (Random House), 1990.

Slonim, Shlomo. "The Electoral College at Philadelphia: The Evolution of an Ad Hoc Congress for the Selection of a President." *Journal of American History* 73, no. 1 (June 1986): 35–58.

Szekely, Kalman S., ed. *Electoral College: A Selective Annotated Bibliography*. Littleton, CO: Libraries Unites, 1970.

BOOKS ABOUT THE CONSTITUTIONAL CONVENTION AND THE FOUNDING FATHERS

Beeman, Richard. *Plain, Honest Men: The Making of the American Constitution*. New York: Random House, 2009.

Berkin, Carol. *A Brilliant Solution: Inventing the American Constitution*. New York and San Diego: Harcourt, 2002.

Bowen, Catherine Drinker. *Miracle at Philadelphia: The Story of the Constitutional Convention, May to September 1787*. Boston: Atlantic Monthly Press, 1966.

Broadwater, Jeff. *James Madison: Son of Virginia and a Founder of the Nation*. Chapel Hill: University of North Carolina Press, 2012.

Brookhiser, Richard. *Gentleman Revolutionary: Gouverneur Morris, the Rake Who Wrote the Constitution*. New York: Free Press, 2003.

Brookhiser, Richard. *James Madison*. New York: Basic Books, 2011.

Cheney, Lynne. *James Madison: A Life Reconsidered*. New York: Viking Penguin, 2014.

Chernow, Ron. *Alexander Hamilton*. New York: Penguin Press, 2004.

Ellis, Joseph J. *The Quartet: Orchestrating the Second American Revolution, 1783–1789*. New York: Knopf, 2015.

Ketcham, Ralph Louis. *James Madison: A Biography*. Charlottesville: University of Virginia Press, (1971) 1990.

Larson, Edward J. *The Return of George Washington 1783–1789*. New York: William Morrow/HarperCollins, 2014.

Maier, Pauline. *Ratification: The People Debate the Constitution, 1787–1788*. New York: Simon & Schuster, 2010.

Rakove, Jack N. *James Madison and the Creation of the American Republic*. Boston: Addison Wesley Longman, (1990) 2001.

Stewart, David O. *The Summer of 1787*. New York: Simon & Schuster, 2007.

Wood, Gordon S., *The Creation of the American Republic 1776–1787*, Chapel Hill: University of North Carolina Press, 1969.

BOOKS ABOUT THE 1800 AND 1824 ELECTIONS

Cunningham, Noble E., Jr. *The Jeffersonian Republicans: The Formation of Party Organization, 1789–1801*. Chapel Hill: University of North Carolina Press, 1958.

Dunn, Susan. *Jefferson's Second Revolution: The Election of 1800 and the Triumph of Republicanism*. Boston: Houghton Mifflin, 2004.

Elkins, Stanley, and Eric McKitrick. *The Age of Federalism*. New York and Oxford: Oxford University Press, 1993.

Heidler, David S., and Jeanne T. Heidler. *Henry Clay: The Essential American*. New York: Random House, 2010.

Horn, James, Jan Lewis, and Peter Onuf. *The Revolution of 1800: Democracy, Race and the Republic*. Charlottesville: University of Virginia Press, 2002.

Kaplan, Fred. *John Quincy Adams: American Visionary*. New York: HarperCollins, 2014.

Knight, Lucian Lamar. *Reminiscences of Famous Georgians*. Atlanta: Franklin-Turner, 1907 (contains a short chapter on William Crawford).

Larson, Edward J. *A Magnificent Catastrophe: The Tumultuous Election of 1800, America's First Presidential Campaign*. New York: Free Press, 2007.

Levin, Phyllis Lee. *The Remarkable Education of John Quincy Adams*. New York: Palgrave Macmillan, 2015.

Parsons, Lynn Hudson. *The Birth of Modern Politics: Andrew Jackson, John Quincy Adams, and the Election of 1828*. New York and Oxford: Oxford University Press, 2009.

Remini, Robert V. *Andrew Jackson*. New York: Harper-Perennial, (1966) 1999.

———. *John Quincy Adams*. New York: Times Books (Henry Holt), 2002.

Schlesinger, Arthur M., ed. *The Coming to Power: Critical Elections in American History*. New York: Chelsea House (McGraw Hill), 1971.

Weston, Florence. *The Presidential Election of 1828*. Washington, DC: Ruddick, 1938.

Wilentz, Sean. *Andrew Jackson*. New York: Times Books (Henry Holt), 2005.

BOOKS ABOUT THE 1876 AND 1888 ELECTIONS

Brodsky, Alyn. *Grover Cleveland: A Study in Character*. New York: St. Martin's Press, 2000.

Burnham, W. Dean. *Presidential Ballots, 1836–1892*. Baltimore: Johns Hopkins University Press, 1955.

Calhoun, Charles W. *Benjamin Harrison*. New York: Times Books, 2005.

———. *Minority Victory: Gilded Age Politics and the Front Porch Campaign of 1888*. Lawrence: University Press of Kansas, 2008.

Ellis, Captain Franklin. *History of Columbia County, New York*. Philadelphia: Everts & Ensign, 1878 (contains a major 1877 speech by Samuel Tilden).

Flick, Alexander C. *Samuel Jones Tilden: A Study in Political Sagacity*. New York: Dodd, Mead, 1939.

Gibson, A. M. *A Political Crime: The History of the Great Fraud*. New York: William S. Gottsberger, 1969.

Graff, Henry F. *Grover Cleveland*. New York: Times Books (Henry Holt), 2002.

Haworth, Paul L. *The Hayes-Tilden Disputed Election of 1876*. New York: Russell & Russell, (1906) 1966.

Hoogenboom, Ari. *Rutherford B. Hayes: Warrior and President.* Lawrence: University of Kansas Press, 1995.

Jeffers, H. Paul. *An Honest President: The Life and Presidencies of Grover Cleveland.* New York: William Morrow, 2000.

Morgan, H. Wayne. *From Hayes to McKinley: National Party Politics, 1877–1896.* Syracuse, NY: Syracuse University Press, 1969.

Morris, Roy, Jr. *Fraud of the Century: Rutherford B. Hayes, Samuel Tilden, and the Stolen Election of 1876.* New York: Simon & Schuster, 2003.

Nevins, Allan. *Grover Cleveland: A Study in Courage.* New York: Dodd, Mead, 1932.

Polakoff, Keith Ian. *The Politics of Inertia: The Election of 1876 and the End of Reconstruction.* Baton Rouge: Louisiana State Press, 1973.

Rehnquist, William H. *Centennial Crisis: The Disputed Election of 1876.* New York: Knopf, 2004.

Robinson, Lloyd. *The Stolen Election: Hayes versus Tilden—1876.* New York: Tom Doherty Associates, (1968) 2001.

Rosenbloom, Eugene H., and Alfred E. Eckes, Jr. *A History of Presidential Elections from George Washington to Jimmy Carter.* New York: Macmillan, 1979.

Schlesinger, Arthur M., Jr., ed. *The Coming to Power, Critical Elections in American History.* New York: Chelsea House (McGraw Hill), 1971.

Schlesinger, Arthur M., Jr., and Fred L. Israel, eds. *History of American Presidential Elections 1876–2001*, vols. 1 and 2. Philadelphia: Chelsea House Publishers, 2002.

Sievers, Harry J. *Benjamin Harrison: Hoosier Statesman, From the Civil War to the White House, 1865–1888.* Newtown, CT: American Political Biography Press, (1959) 1996.

Smith, Marie, and Louise Durbin. *White House Brides.* Washington, DC: Acropolis Books, 1966 (contains a chapter on Frances Folsom Cleveland).

Socolofsky, Homer E., and Allan B. Spetter. *The Presidency of Benjamin Harrison.* Lawrence: University of Kansas Press, 1987.

Summers, Mark Wahlgren. *Rum, Romanism and Rebellion: The Making of a President, 1884.* Chapel Hill: University of North Carolina Press, 2000.

Wallace, Lew. *Life of Gen. Ben Harrison.* Charleston, SC: BiblioBazaar, (1888) 2008.

Williams, Charles R. *The Life of Rutherford B. Hayes.* Boston: Houghton Mifflin, 1914.

BOOKS ABOUT THE 1968 ELECTION

Aitken, Jonathan. *Nixon, A Life.* Washington, DC: Regnery, 1993.

Carter, Dan T. *The Politics of Rage: George Wallace, the Origins of the New Conservatism, and the Transformation of American Politics.* New York: Simon & Schuster, 1995.

Chester, Lewis, Godfrey Hodgson, and Bruce Page. *An American Melodrama: The Presidential Campaign of 1968.* New York: Viking, 1969.

Edsall, Thomas Byrne, and Mary D. Edsall. *Chain Reaction: The Impact of Race, Rights and Taxes on American Politics.* New York: W. W. Norton, 1991.

English, David. *Divided They Stand.* Englewood Cliffs, NJ: Prentice-Hall, 1969.

Frady, Marshall. *Wallace.* New York: Random House, (1968) 1996.

Gould, Lewis L. *1968: The Election That Changed America.* Chicago: Ivan R. Dee, 2010.

Humphrey, Hubert H. *The Education of a Public Man.* New York: Doubleday, 1976.

Kearns, Doris. *Lyndon Johnson and the American Dream.* New York: St. Martin's Griffin, (1976) 1991.

Nixon, Richard. *RN: The Memoirs of Richard Nixon.* New York: Grosset & Dunlap, 1978.

Phillips, Kevin P. *The Emerging Republican Majority.* Garden City, NY: Anchor Books (Doubleday), 1970.

Tillman, Barrett. *LeMay.* New York: Palgrave Macmillan, 2007.

Wallace, George C. *Stand Up For America.* New York: Doubleday, 1976.

White, Theodore H. *The Making of a President 1968.* New York: Atheneum, 1969.

BOOKS ABOUT THE 2000 ELECTION

Danner, Mark. *The Road to Illegitimacy.* Hoboken, NJ: Melville House, 2004.

Dershowitz, Alan. *Supreme Injustice: How the High Court Hijacked Election 2000.* New York and Oxford: Oxford University Press, 2001.

Dionne, E. J., and William Kristol, eds. *Bush v. Gore: The Court Cases and the Commentary.* Washington, DC: Brookings Institution Press, 2001.

Dover, E. D. *The Disputed Presidential Election of 2000.* Westport, CT: Greenwood Press, 2002.

Jacobson, Gary C. *The 2000 Elections and Beyond.* Washington, DC: CQ Press, 2001.

Kaplan, David A. *The Accidental President.* New York: HarperCollins, 2001.

Posner, Richard A. *Breaking the Deadlock: The 2000 Election, the Constitution, and the Courts*. Princeton, NJ: Princeton University Press, 2001.

Rakove, Jack N., ed. *The Unfinished Election of 2000*. New York: Basic Books, 2001.

Toobin, Jeffrey. *Too Close to Call: The Thirty-Six-Day Battle to Decide the 2000 Election*. New York: Random House, 2001.

Zelden, Charles L. *Bush v. Gore: Exposing the Hidden Crisis in American Democracy*. Lawrence: University Press of Kansas, 2008.

BOOKS ABOUT VOTING IN THE ROMAN REPUBLIC

Botsford, George W. *The Roman Assemblies: From Their Origin to the End of the Republic*. Lanham, MD: Cooper Square, (1909) 1968.

Taylor, Lily Ross. *Party Politics in the Age of Caesar*. Berkeley: University of California Press, (1949) 1968.

———. *Roman Voting Assemblies: From the Hannibalic War to the Dictatorship of Caesar*. Ann Arbor: University of Michigan Press, (1966) 1993.

Index

Adams, John
  avoiding war with France, 64–65, 69–70
  comparisons with Jefferson, 65–68
  election of 1796, 5–6, 15–16, 64, 66
  election of 1800 controversy and
    resolution, 69–77
  end of presidency, 71, 75–76
  greatest mistake of presidency, 65–66
  offering Jefferson presidency deal, 74
  Sedition Act and, 65, 66
  in White House, 75–76
  winner-take-all origins and, 5–6
  working with Jefferson, 66
Adams, John Quincy. *See also* election
    (1824)
  birth, family background, early years,
    80–81
  election of 1824, 88–93
  election of 1828, 93–94
  expanding US territory, 86
  marriage to Louisa Johnson, 81
  as one of four presidential
    candidates, 79
  parental expectations/influences, 80, 81
  political background/positions, 80, 81–82
  winning presidency, 92–93
Agnew, Spiro, 111, 115, 163
Albert, Carl, 163–64
Arthur, Chester A., 49–50

Bayard, James, 74–75, 82
Bedford, Gunning, Jr., 120
Bell, John, 196, 197, 198
Bennett, Robert, 130
Best, Judith, 123
Biden, Joe, 17–18, 135

Black vote
  15th Amendment granting rights, 37
  Civil Rights Act of 1875 and, 45
  Civil Rights Act of 1964 and, 95
  District Plan and, 125
  efforts to suppress, 38, 56, 100
  election 2000 and, 22–23
  election of 1876 and, 38, 44–45
  election of 1888 and, 56–57
  election of 1968 and, 95–97, 102, 111
  electoral system impact, 137
  equal protection and, 36
  Harrison working for rights, 58
  Voting Rights Act of 1965 and, 95
  winner-take-all system and, 137–38
Blaine, James G., 37–38, 50, 53, 54, 196
Bonus Plan, 123
Breaking the Deadlock (Posner), 24
Breckinridge, John, 196, 197, 198
Bryan, Guy, 35
Bryan, William Jennings, 60, 67
Burchard, Samuel, 53
Burr, Aaron
  campaign prowess of, 68–69
  as Jefferson opponent, ensuing
    controversy/resolution, 69–77
  as Jefferson running mate, 63
  Jefferson's opinion of, 72
Bush, George W. *See* election (2000);
    election (2004)
busing, court-ordered, 97, 102, 111, 114

Calhoun, John, 9, 86, 88, 92
Canal Ring, 33
Carmichael, Stokely, 96
Carter, Jimmy, 4, 17, 126, 195

208

About the Author

Mark Weston grew up in Armonk, New York, and worked as a lawyer for ABC Television and as a journalist for ABC News before writing five books, including *Prophets and Princes, Saudi Arabia from Muhammad to the Present*, and *Giants of Japan: The Lives of Japan's Greatest Men and Women*. He has written articles for the *New York Times*, the *Washington Post*, and the *Los Angeles Times* and has appeared on CNN. He has also written a play, *Meet George Orwell*, that has been performed at colleges and presidential libraries. A graduate of Brown University and the University of Texas Law School, he lives in Sarasota, Florida, with his wife, painter Linda Richichi.